TOP GEAR: 1977-2015:

2000 COPY LIMITED EDITION

ISBN-13: 978-1512312904

ISBN-10: 1512312908

Also by the Author:

TROJAN LAW FOR SECURITY OFFICERS (2013)
(Retired)

LAW & PRACTICE FOR SECURITY PROFESSIONALS
(2013)

COLLECTION EDITIONS: TOP GEAR (2014)

COLLECTION EDITIONS: NCIS (2014)

COLLECTION EDITIONS: MERCEDES IN FORMULA
ONE (2014)

COLLECTION EDITIONS: GAME OF THRONES; An
Inside Guide to the Hit Show (2014)

COLLECTION EDITIONS: SPACE SHUTTLE (2015)

COLLECTION EDITIONS: THE WALKING DEAD: An
Inside Guide to the Hit Show (2015)

COLLECTION EDITIONS: FERRARI IN FORMULA
ONE (2015)

First Printing: 2015

Top Gear: 1977 – 2015:

Limited Edition - 2000

This book is one of a maximum 2000 copies printed worldwide.

Contents

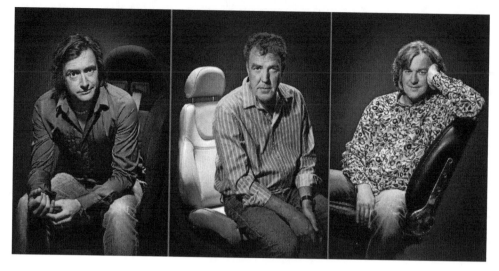

Foreword

And so we have it... Top Gear... The most watched factual television programme in the history of mankind.

Starting as a simple motoring magazine show in the late 70's, Top Gear grew into the huge phenomena that we see and love today. Its, not so subtle, blend of controversy, informative (and sometimes not so informative) news, quirky car reviews, and outrageous challenges made the show totally unique in the world of television. Never before had a factual show dared to push the boundaries of entertainment with a total disregard for the views and opinions of anyone other than its fans. Perhaps that is why the show had become so popular? That unique vision and ambition to satisfy the needs of so many fans without the worries of "will we offend anybody who doesn't watch us and do we care"?

Top Gear now features on the television schedules of fifty-five countries around the globe and has a global audience of more than 350 million regular viewers (and that is just the U.K. version of the show). Top Gear has become an integral part of family life on a Sunday evening.

Sadly 2015 was the year for Top Gear, as we know it, to come to its sad end. The controversy that had made the show so popular finally became the reason for its demise. The future of the show... who knows? No doubt another format of the show will reappear but as for the likes of Clarkson, May, and Hammond? That era has sadly come to an end. But let us not regret... Let us look back and remember the past 37 years of fun.

Introduction

The year is 1977... Friday April 22nd... Simon Peres becomes Premier of Israel, orchestra leader Charles Sanford dies at the age of 71 and, at 22:15 on BBC 1, The Allman Brothers Band play 'Jessica' as Angela Rippon and Tom Coyne present a brand new motoring show on BBC Midlands... Top Gear.

This innovative new show is far from the 'laughs & jollies' show that we all know and love today. There is no Stig, no amphibious vehicles, and a 200+ mph supercar is far from the imaginations of most viewer's minds. The original shows format came from the mind of Executive Producer Derek Smith and was shown on the television sets of Midland region viewers only. The idea being... a monthly, half hour, 'magazine' style show previewing new cars, road safety, holiday touring, fuel economy and other motoring events which would clearly make todays avid viewer yawn consistently. The reason it was shown around Birmingham? Well in the 70's, believe it or not, Britain had a thriving car manufacturing industry. Much of this was based around the Midlands area and so it was thought that this being the 'Motoring Central' of Great Britain, there might be a few car enthusiasts interested in the show.

The first episodes main feature was by presenter, Angela Rippon, as she drove in her Ford Capri, from Shepherds Bush, in London, to the Top Gear studio at Pebble Mill in Birmingham giving reports on driving conditions and the cost of food at service stations during the course of her journey. Top Gear's very first presenter also kindly pointed out that 'mirrors' on cars were very useful for looking behind you on the motorway. If the show's first viewers were unsure on these new-fangled mirror things, Ms. Rippon also demonstrated where on the vehicle these were located. A rear view mirror on the windscreen and two further mirrors attached as one to the driver's door and one to the passengers door. How educational?!

Further features on the show contained reports on fuel economy, road signs and an interview with the then Transport Minister. Nine episodes later, and the first season came to an end. But had it been a success??

1977 Top Gear

Angela Rippon OBE was born 12th October 1944 and presented radio and television news programs in the South West of England before becoming the first female journalist to present the Nine O'clock news on BBC in 1975. She up scaled from the news briefly to present Top Gear from 1977 to 1979. I could continue to tell you of her early life growing up in Plymouth, Devon. Perhaps go on to tell you more of the early years in her career, her children's books, her work as Chairman of the English National Ballet?? But to be fair… we are only at the beginning of this book and I would like you to continue reading further.

Tom Coyne. We don't know when he was born or anything of interest about him. Tom Coyne was the front man of 'Midlands Today' and presented more than 4000 episodes. Midlands Today was a local evening news programme filmed in Birmingham. He presented the local first series of Top Gear along with Angela and has not been heard or seen of since.

BBC MIDLANDS TELEVISION

1978 – 1987 Top Gear

Well the show must have shown some sign of promise, despite its lack of exciting topics. The BBC decided to make Top Gear a weekly, 30 minute, format to be shown on BBC2 across the country from July of 1978. Its creator, Derek Smith, remained with the show as its Executive Producer and Angela Rippon stayed for a further year to give further invaluable motoring advice, almost as important as the location of the mirrors.

New topics were added to the show to make it more interesting to the now wider audience and included information on MOT's and rust and corrosion prevention. Angela's drive from one place to another, whilst describing the traffic/weather/food on the way, must have been a success as it was retained for the new series as "Rippon on the Road".

Some slightly more interesting topics covered rush hour traffic over the holiday weekends, tachographs in HGV's, coverage of the British Motor Show and the Lombard RAC Rally.

Although Angela Rippon only remained with the show until 1979, the second incarnation of Top Gear expanded to include a number of other presenters including William Woollard and Noel Edmonds with co-presenters Barrie Gill, Sue Baker, Judith Jackson, Frank Page and Chris Goffrey.

Noel Edmonds is a much loved television and radio producer and the son of a Headmaster. His first presenting position was on Radio Luxembourg in 1968, a position he got by sending recordings he had made of himself to offshore radio stations. After a year with Radio Luxembourg, Noel moved back to the UK and joined Radio 1 as a 'fill-in' radio presenter before getting a two-hour Saturday afternoon slot of his own in 1970.

Noel Edmonds then went on to present a number of other television and radio shows in the United Kingdom such as Top of the Pops, the Eurovision Song Contest and Juke Box Jury before presenting Top Gear through the 1980's. He also briefly returned for a one off special of Top Gear in 1990 to road test an original 1960's Ford GT40 when it was found that the then host, a Mr. Jeremy Clarkson, at 6 ft. 5 in was in fact too tall to fit in the car.

Mr. Noel Edmonds was also responsible for the very first controversial subject on Top Gear when he described the Fiat Strada by saying it "wasn't very good" because of its poor paint colour and the electrical wiring hanging from under the dashboard. Fiat threatened to sue the BBC unless he apologized for the reference. Needless to say, journalistic integrity ruled and no apology was made, but on a later date, Noel visited another car show. When he walked up to the Fiat stage to do his report, Fiat staff immediately moved him off because of his poor comment regarding their Strada. At that time it must have been considered rude to give a negative report when reviewing a product. How things have changed on Top Gear since.

Noel's daughter recently witnessed an old episode of Top Gear which was being presented by her father, with his trademark beard and thick hair. She responded to this by running to her mother and informing her that there was a 'lady' on television that looked just like dad.

William Woollard originally trained as a fighter pilot with the RAF after attending Oxford University. He had also worked as a Social Scientist studying social responsibility with a number of American and European organizations before entering into a television career with the BBC as a writer, presenter and producer.

Perhaps his best remembered role was as producer and presenter of 'Tomorrow's World' on the BBC for 11 years, but William's also presented Top Gear for almost 10 years (1981 -1991) as well as the 'Rally Report' which covered the Lombard RAC Rally.

Since his time on Top Gear William Woollard has produced and presented a number of documentaries for the BBC, Channel 4, National Geographic, and the Discovery Channel and has written a book based upon his beliefs as a Buddhist.

1987 – 2001 Rein-Car-Nation

In 1987, Top Gear claimed a new producer to work alongside the current producer, Ken Pollock. His name was Jon Bentley. Jon saw potential in the programme and understand that the shows rather bland set up needed to be addressed. At this time both producers set about trying to make the show a little more humorous and hired a number of new presenters. These presenters included Tom Boswell, Tony Mason and an ex Formula 1 driver named Tiff Needell. Also added to the line-up was a little known Journalist from Performance Car Magazine… Jeremy Clarkson.

This new line up and look to the series soon stood proud. The show gained a massive audience increase and within a year Top Gear had become BBC2's most viewed programme, drawing in around 5 million viewers despite receiving regular criticism for being a little environmentally unfriendly and perhaps, on occasion, encouraging slightly irresponsible driving. It is good to see those issues have been addressed in the current series.

Jon Bentley is a television presenter and producer, mostly specializing in motoring issues. He is perhaps best recognized as a co-presenter of Channel 5's 'The Gadget Show'. Jon was a producer of Top Gear from 1987 until 1999 when he defected (along with the production crew and presenters) to Channel 5's 'Fifth Gear' from 2002 – 2004. Since that time, Jon has presented the Gadget Show until that show was re-formatted in early 2012. Plans are underway to develop the Gadget Show back to its original format in the future and so Mr. Bentley could well be back on out screens in no time.

Ken Pollock was a teacher of Agricultural Engineering at Newcastle University before becoming a television producer with the BBC. He began producing the BBC's farming programs in the 70's before joining Top Gear in 1987, along with Jeremy Clarkson. Ken also created the series 'Top Gear Motorsport' which was presented by Tiff Needell.

Ken eventually left the BBC to become an independent television producer dealing mainly with Motorsports programs. He now works in local government as Chairman of West Worcestershire Conservatives.

Tom Boswell worked in both radio and television as a Journalist and Presenter in the 80's. Tom began his Top Gear Curriculum Vitae by presenting two episodes of Top Gear in 1981 & 1982. Then between 1988 & 1990 he returned to present another 20 episodes on such topics as car theft and motorcycles. Sadly, Tom passed away in 1990.

Tony Mason is probably one of the best recognized faces from the original Top Gear series. Even today he carries his mischievous looks and trademark cap honorably. Tony began his career as a successful rally co-driver. He has navigated a win and two 2nd place results for Roger Clark in the RAC rally in the 1970's (being the only British crew to have done so in over 35 years). As well as being a navigator, Tony has also taken to the controls himself and proved a highly competent rally driver. Even today, Tony still competes in Classic Rally's.

Tony Mason officially retired from professional Rallying in the mid 80's and turned, naturally, to television presenting. He became one of Top Gears longest running presenters on the show (between 1986 and 2000). Tony's specialty on the show was, unsurprisingly, Motorsport. He also presented regular features on HGV's, Fire Engines, Buses and Vintage Rolls Royce. Mr. Mason also holds the current record on Top Gear for having tested the most expensive vehicle on the show – a £15 million concept bus by Volvo. Today Tony continues to present television pro-grams, most recently 'Off the Road' & 'Classic Car Club' for Sky Discovery. He also writes regular Motorsports articles for magazines and newspapers and works as an after-dinner speaker.

Tiff Needell achieved an honour's degree in Civil engineering at City University, London, before commencing employment as a Structural Design Engineer. It was at this time that he fell in love with racing.

Tiff's first race was at Brands Hatch in 1970, when he attended a driving school. As luck would have it, Tiff was able to continue this new found passion for racing when he won his first race car in an Autosport magazine competition. A Lotus 69 FF. From here, he eventually bought an Elden Mk10 and then a Crossle 25F. It was in the Crossle that Tiff was noticed. He entered the Kent Messenger FF Championship, halfway through its official season, and went onto win. This landed him a paid drive in the Formula Ford 2000 Championship. Tiff's success in Formula Ford catapulted him into Formula 3 and then the British Formula One Championship which also saw multiple successes.

In 1979, Tiff moved into World Formula One but after it turned out he had the wrong racing license he had to forfeit the year. Tiff returned to World Formula One in 1980, this time with the correct license, and raced for the 'Ensign' race team.

The late 80's saw Tiff move into British Rallycross in a Metro 6R4, finishing 4th in his very first Rallycross event. After a couple of years in British Rallycross, Tiff entered the 24 hours at LeMans. He competed in this grueling race a number of times driving an Ibec Hesketh 308LM, an Aston Martin Nimrod NRA/C2, a Porsche 956, and a Aston Martin EMKA C84/1.

In 1987 Tiff began presenting on Top Gear and his need to push the cars past their limits proved a particular success and popular with the shows viewers. Tiff continued to not only present Top Gear until its first demise in 2001, but also continued to race in Daytona, driving Porsche and Lister Storm's and again LeMans in a Jaguar XJ220.

In 2001, Needell moved (along with the majority of production crew and presenters) to Channel 5 to present Top Gear's remake as Fifth Gear. Tiff continues to present this show today, although it is now shown on Discovery Channel after it was recently dropped by Channel 5. Tiff's connection with Top Gear has never fully been repealed though. He still writes for 'Top Gear Magazine' and in 2003 to 2006 he co-presented the Top Gear Live show at Earls Court. He has also appeared in the 2005 Top Gear Comic Relief special 'Stars in Fast Cars' and appeared again in Top Gear in 2010 as the 'Emergency Stig', training Slumdog Millionaire Director Danny Boyle for the shows 'Star in a Reasonably Priced Car' (after the show's original Stig (Ben Collins) was controversially fired after writing his autobiography) and again in 2011, pretending to be James May whilst driving the Ariel Atom V8 around the Top Gear test track.

Jeremy Clarkson is considered by many to be the 'embodiment of Top Gear'. Jeremy is a Doncaster lad, born to a Mum and Dad. These two, probably loving, parents were Edward Grenville Clarkson (a travelling salesman) and Shirley Gabrielle Ward (a teacher). Both it appears were rather handy with needles and cotton as they also dabbled in the production and selling of tea cozies and, later, Paddington Bears, which not only paid for Jeremy's private schooling but also provided an income later in life as Jeremy's first paid job was selling these bears.

Jeremy Clarkson's early years involved him being expelled from Repton School in Doncaster, as he portrays it, for apparently "smoking, drinking, and making a nuisance of himself". Also attending Repton School at this time (although lasting longer there) was Formula One designer Adrian Newey. Mr. Newey went on to win nine Formula One Constructors Championships, an OBE, and is now Chief Technical Officer of Red Bull Racing.

Jeremy has been married twice and currently lives in a very big house in the Cotswold's with his wife and three daughters. Jeremy is known to complain about the number of 'boy racers' (or 'prats' as we would also know them) who know of his address and enjoy nothing more than revving there Astra diesels outside his house, we can only assume that they are hoping Jeremy will be wildly impressed and go outside to offer them a job co-presenting Top Gear... or maybe not.

One of Jeremy's greatest achievements is his dress sense. His well known, and much admired, suit jacket and jeans fashion has become a 'must wear' amongst many celebrities and has affectionately became known as 'the Jeremy Clarkson effect'.

The 90's continued to go well for Top Gear. The show maintained its popularity and grew as a non-biased reporting series. Car manufacturers began to take notice of issues presented in the show. No longer would manufacturers threaten to sue at every bad comment made towards their cars. They understood that Top Gear reports could have a serious impact on sales as the show influenced its viewers buying opinions.

The 90's also brought about the introduction of a number of other presenters, notably including Quentin Wilson, Michele Newman, Steve Berry, Vicki Butler-Henderson, Brendan Coogan and briefly a certain James May.

Quentin Wilson is the son of Professor Bernard Wilson. Prof. Wilson (Senior) was the first code breaker to break the Italian Navy Hagelin C-35 Code Machine during the Second World War. Quentin followed in his father's academic background at first by studying English Literature at the University of Leicester before opening his first used car dealership, selling nothing less than Ferraris and Maserati's.

In 1991 Quentin began as a Co-Presenter on Top Gear and featured in every episode over the following decade, offering invaluable advice on Used Cars. After 'Top Gears' demise in 2001, Quentin moved (along with almost everybody else) to Channel 5. Here he began co-presenting 'Fifth Gear'. After a brief spell on this show, Quentin began producing for channel 5. Since then it appears to have almost all gone well for Quentin as he has successfully created a number of documentaries for the channel including 'Britain's Worst Driver', 'Britain's Worst Mother', 'Britain's Worst DIYer', 'Britain's Worst Husband', 'Britain's Worst Teenager', 'Britain's Worst Builder' and 'Britain's Worst Zookeeper'. It has not all been plain sailing however as in 2002, Quentin participated in 'Strictly Come Dancing' and was voted off after only one dance with the shows lowest ever score. Quentin was described by then host, Craig Revel-Horwood, as "Britain's worst Dancer".

Michelle Newman graduated from the University of York before commencing employment at the 'Liverpool Echo' newspaper. Michelle later lived in Italy and France teaching English as a private tutor.

In 1983, Michelle began her presenting career on the Regional News programme 'Look East in Norwich' before moving to the 'Central News' programme in Birmingham six years later. From 1993 to 1998 we watched Ms. Newman co-presenting Top Gear. Her good looks and quintessential manner made her far more interesting than Angela Rippon. Whilst working on Top Gear,  Michelle also presented live political de-bates and a motoring magazine for ITV called 'Pulling Power'.

Since then, Michelle has run her own production company 'Newman Productions' and has studied Mandarin Chinese at the School of African and Oriental Studies in London and Beijing.

Steve Berry has produced and presented numerous motoring shows over the years, including of course Top Gear and later the 'Top Gear Motor-sport' and 'Top Gear Radio Show' spinoffs.

Barry is probably best known for his love of motorcycles and has written and presented a number of shows since leaving Top Gear including 'Bennett's Biker Build Off' for the Discovery Channel and 'The Bikes, The Stars' for the BBC. Barry has also hosted phone-in shows and presented radio shows and now writes for 'The Sunday Times' and 'Classic Car Weekly'.

Vicki Butler-Henderson comes from racing pedigree. Her Grandfather used to race at Brooklands in a classic 'Frazer Nash' and her father was in the British Karting Team. Her Brother is also a racing driver. It was no surprise then, that a young Vicki started racing Karts at the young age of 12. In her first race she was overtaken by, a then also unknown, David Coulthard. Since that time Vicki has gone on to gain her car race license as well as a power boat race license.

Vicki began her career as a journalist for 'Auto Express', 'Performance Car', 'Max Power', and 'What Car' magazines whilst also supplementing her income as a racing instructor at Silverstone racing circuit.

Vicki co-presented Top Gear from 1997 until the show was cancelled in 2001. From there, Vicki moved to Channel 5's 'Fifth Gear' and still presents it now. Vicki has also presented radio shows for 'Virgin Radio' and other television shows for ITV as well as various 'voice overs' for advertisements such as 'Wrigley's' chewing gum and 'Sony'. Vicki was also a voiceover for the 'Gran Turismo 4' game on the PlayStation 2.

Vicki is currently married to Phil Churchward. Phil is the Top Gear series director.

Brendan Coogan presented Top Gear in the mid 90's and is brother to comedian Steve Coogan and 'Mock Turtles' singer Martin Coogan. As well as boasting two rather well known brothers and co-presenting Top Gear, Brendan has also been a presenter on Radio 5, Radio Manchester and Sky One motoring show 'Vroom Vroom'.

James May co-presented Top Gear in 1999 and then joined the 'New Top Gear' in its second season and remains an integral part of the show's popularity.

After studying music at Lancaster University, May worked as a Records Officer in a hospital in Chelsea before commencing a journalistic career with 'The Engineer' magazine and later 'Autocar'. James was dismissed from Autocar magazine after putting a hidden message in one edition of the

magazine which he did not expect anybody to notice. Unfortunately a number of readers did as they quickly phoned the magazine thinking they had won a prize for deciphering James's hidden message.

James had to create a spread featuring various reviews. Each review began with a large red letter. With the red letters in order they read "So you think it's really good, yeah? You should try making the bloody thing up; it's a real pain in the arse".

Despite James's nickname of 'Captain Slow', he has in fact done some pretty amazing acts. In Season 9 James drove a Bugatti Veyron to its top speed of 253 mph (407 km/h) and then in a later episode he took the Veyron's big brother (the Bugatti Veyron Supersport) to 260 mph (417 km/h). In one of the teams many brilliant challenges, Jeremy Clarkson described an amazing achievement made by May…

"the first person to go there, who didn't want to be there" … *Clarkson & May's drive by car to the Magnetic North Pole.*

The First End??

Despite Top Gear's huge popularity over the previous 23 years, 2000 proved to see further the shows decline. Viewing figures slumped from around 6 million to less than 3 million. It appeared, for all intense purposes, that the show had outlived its welcome. In 2001, after many of the shows crew and presenters had already jumped ship, the BBC decided to pull the plug on Top Gear. They did make one further 'special episode' in 2002 which had coverage of the Birmingham Motor Show but despite good viewing of this the show was at an end...

Or so we thought...

Fifth Gear

The 'not quite so popular' Fifth Gear featured on Channel 5 from 2002. It has been considered the nearest rival to Top Gear, but it is in fact simply a reincarnation of the original Top Gear.

The promise of Top Gears potential was observed closely by another television channel in 2002, this time in Channel 5 as they realized that giving the show a facelift may recover those declining audiences. Channel 5 not only decided to relaunch Top Gear, but also took with them most of the shows production team including producer Tom Bentley. They also signed up former Top Gear presenters Vicki Butler-Henderson, Tiff Needell, Quentin Wilson and Adrian Simpson to present the newly formatted version of Top Gear.

The only part of the show the BBC refused to relinquish was its title... The name Top Gear was still being used by the BBC as the title of its accompanying magazine and so the BBC, wanting no affiliation with Channel 5's version of the series, refused to hand over the title. Instead, Channel 5 used a little initiative and titled the series 'Fifth Gear'. Smart thinking!!

2002 – Present

Jeremy Clarkson and, producer, Andy Wilman approached the BBC with the intention of reformatting the Top Gear series. They believed the show had potential and simply required a few "tweaks". The British Broadcasting Corporation, thankfully liked the idea and took a chance. In 2002 the new series was launched. The new series brought in a steady three presenters rather than the habble dabble of before. A "home" for Top Gear was also purchased at the Dunsfold Aerodrome in Waverley, Surrey. A disused hanger made the perfect studio and the airports taxiways and runways had, by pure chance, already been set up as a testing track by Lotus. The introduction of a "tame racing driver" to test cars was also brought in with the Stig. New segments were also introduced such as the "Star in a Reasonably Priced Car", "Power Laps", "The News" and later on "The Cool Wall" as well as various other challenges.

Jason Dawe was born and raised in Cornwall, England and has worked in the motoring industry most of his life. He co-presented the newly revised Top Gear for the show's first season. Jason's specialty was in bargain cars and buying second hand. Jason continues to work today as a motoring writer for the Sunday Times and other motoring magazines. He has also co-hosted the Used Car Roadshow

Richard Hammond was born on the 19th of December, 1969, in Solihull, Warwickshire. He began his presenting career as a DJ on Radio Cleveland, Radio York,  Radio Cumbria, Radio Leeds, Radio Newcastle and Radio Lancashire before moving to television where he presented a car show called "Motoring Week" on the Men & Motors channel. Richard has since co-presented new Top Gear since its revision in 2002. As well as this, "the Hamster" has since presented almost everything else on British Television including Braniac-Science Abuse, his own short-lived daytime chat show (the Richard Hammonds 5 o'clock show), the 2005 Cruft's dog show, Total Wipeout, several hundred documentaries on earth and science and has fronted a series of advertisements for a well-known supermarket. Richard also had the opportunity to interview his childhood hero Evel Knievel in 2007 shortly before the famed motorcycle stunt rider passed away.

The Stig. Since the shows relaunch in 2002 there have been three Stig's. The idea of the Stig was down to Clarkson and producer Andi Wilman. The name comes from their Repton School days where new pupils were referred to as "Stig's".

The Stig's introductions on the show have underlined his oddness. Initially the presenters heralded his appearance with simple humorous introductions, such as "His Holiness, the Stig!" Beginning in series 6, the introductions began to follow a format of, "Some say that..."; "All we know is, he's called the Stig."

Characteristics described in this format include:

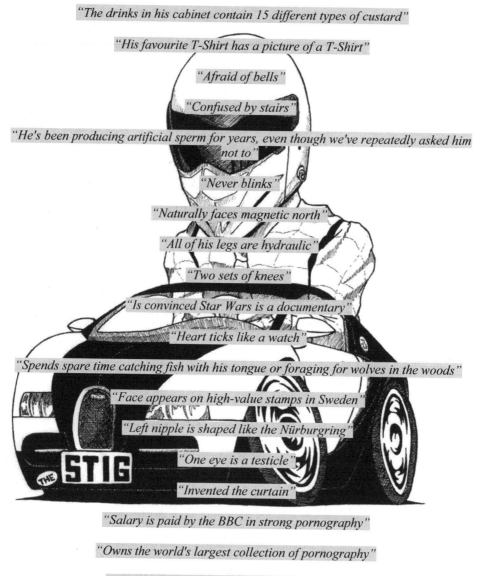

"The drinks in his cabinet contain 15 different types of custard"

"His favourite T-Shirt has a picture of a T-Shirt"

"Afraid of bells"

"Confused by stairs"

"He's been producing artificial sperm for years, even though we've repeatedly asked him not to"

"Never blinks"

"Naturally faces magnetic north"

"All of his legs are hydraulic"

"Two sets of knees"

"Is convinced Star Wars is a documentary"

"Heart ticks like a watch"

"Spends spare time catching fish with his tongue or foraging for wolves in the woods"

"Face appears on high-value stamps in Sweden"

"Left nipple is shaped like the Nürburgring"

"One eye is a testicle"

"Invented the curtain"

"Salary is paid by the BBC in strong pornography"

"Owns the world's largest collection of pornography"

"Developed the "wonderful" scent of Wednesday"

"Only knows two facts about ducks, and both of them are wrong"

"Has a full size tattoo of his face, on his face"

"Has terrible plans involving the Moon"

The first Stig was in fact, racing driver, Perry McCarthy and appeared in 22 Top Gear episodes as the black-suited, original Stig.

Perry McCarthy was born 3rd of March, 1961, and has raced everything from Formula 1 to the LeMans. McCarthy was cast as the Stig following a chance meeting with Jeremy Clarkson at the 2002 launch party for McCarthy's autobiography, 'Flat Out, Flat Broke: Formula 1 the Hard Way'. This led to an audition as a regular presenter, before the production team decided the racing driver should be anonymous.

After the first series ended, an article in The Sunday Mirror on 12th January 2003 named McCarthy as the Stig. After the second series ended, McCarthy published the second edition of his autobiography, in which he confirmed that he was the Stig. McCarthy was then "killed off" in the first episode of the third series. The scene which saw Black Stig "killed off," nicknamed "Top Gun vs Top Gear," was an attempt to race to 100 mph (160 km/h) and then come to a halt on the 200 metre (660ft) long flight deck of HMS Invincible. a Royal Navy aircraft carrier on which British Aerospace Sea Harrier jump jets reach 100 mph (160 km/h) be-fore take-off. He would be using the "old Top Gear Jag," a white Jaguar XJS bought for a "couple of hundred quid," stripped of its fittings and fitted with nitrous injection to take it to 500 bhp. The Stig accelerated along the deck, and an on-screen speedometer indicated 109 mph (175 km/h) before a cutaway shot saw the car flying off the end of the runway ramp and into the sea. Clarkson then revealed in the last scene of the episode that a glove floating on the sea was all that divers had found. Ac-cording to McCarthy, "We tried to make it as much like a scene out of James Bond as possible."

The explanations for McCarthy's exit vary. While McCarthy described the parting as amiable in 2008, The Times claimed in 2009 that he had fallen out with producers. In 2010, McCarthy said he had become tired of the job, which he claimed paid £700 a week, and that part of his annoyance stemmed from an attempt by a car owner to sue him for ruining his car and the BBC's refusal to defend him due to his anonymity. He said the BBC chose not to renew his contract and had him written out of the show.

Although McCarthy said in 2006 that, following his exit from Top Gear, he harbored ambitions of re-entering racing in the Grand Prix Masters series, he went on to run an investment company and appear as an after-dinner speaker.

The second Stig was brought into the show in November 2003. His identity was kept secret until racing driver Ben Collins wrote his auto-biography ('The Man in the White Suit') in August 2010 claiming to be the Stig. The BBC and Ben Collins publishers started legal proceedings against each other, with the BBC attempting to obtain a High Court in-junction to prevent the publishing of the book. The injunction was quashed by the High Court and so the secret was officially out.

Ben Collins was born 13th of February 1975 in Bristol, England. He has competed in motor racing since 1994 in many categories, from Formula Three and Indy Lights to sports cars, GT racing and stock cars.

Collins was placed second in the Marlboro Masters Formula 3 championship event in 2000. He set the pace at the 2001 Le Mans 24 hours race in his first season for approximately four hours during the rain at night. After winning the European Stock Car Championship in 2003 ASCAR stock car racing he was signed by PDM Racing to do selected rounds of the 2004 Indy Racing League, but the car never appeared. In 2005, he competed in the British GT Championship in a Porsche 996 GT3, winning races on the way before moving up to the FIA GT Series with Ascari where he led races and scored several pole positions. After Collins identity came known he was dropped by the BBC and took up position with 'Fifth Gear' as a presenter for season 18. He did not re-appear for the following season 19.

In 2012, Collins joined as co-presenter on Polish TV's 'Automaniak'

The third Stig remains a well-kept secret and remains in the show at present... But for how long???

The Stig's "cousins"

Various episodes have featured "cousins" of the Stig, often when the show is filming outside of the United Kingdom.

In the US Special in 2006, the show featured a portly American cousin nicknamed "Big Rig Stig.". He raced the presenters' cars around the Palm Beach International Raceway track.

The Botswana Special featured the "Stig's African cousin", with dark skin, wearing just Puma racing boots, a loincloth, white racing gloves and the iconic white helmet. He raced two of the presenters' chosen cars around an improvised rally track.

There was another cousin in the Vietnam Special, although his scenes were not broadcast due to time constraints. He was nicknamed the "Stig's Vietnamese/Communist cousin" and wore a red uniform. The foot-age was however included in a later DVD release. Top Gear hired a local motorcycle stunt rider.

In Series 14, episode 2, the Stig's vegetarian cousin, nicknamed "Janet Stig Porter", appeared. He wore green overalls, Birkenstock sandals with socks, and a solar-powered helmet. He drove the presenters' "Hammerhead Eagle iThrust" hybrid around the MIRA test circuit to see how long it would last, but died from the car's diesel fumes.

In Series 15, episode 2, the Stig's German cousin, nicknamed "Herr Stig" and "Stiggy Ray Cyrus", appeared. He was almost identical to the main Stig, the main difference being a mullet haircut. He drove the presenters' cheap sports saloons around EuroSpeedway in Lausitz.

In Series 18 episode 1, the Stig's Italian cousin, "Bunga-Bunga Stig", was introduced during the final leg of their Italian Road Trip at Imola Circuit. He came out of a motor-home dressed in a suit, followed by three glamorous girls, to set a lap time in a Ferrari 458 Italia.

In Series 18 episode 2, the Stig's Chinese cousin "Attack Stig" made his dramatic arrival by kung fu kicking through a door at the local race track. While in appearance he looks the same as the normal Stig, the Chinese Stig is found to be highly violent and attacks indiscriminately with martial arts. His unruly behaviour caused problems not just for the presenters but also for the Top Gear filming crew, flag bearer and a nearby track marshal, the latter of which this Stig even interrupted his timed lap of the Roewe 350 in order to attack. After the timed laps, he walked on-screen and kicked James "in the plums." His behaviour was so bad that Clarkson remarked, "That's the worst Stig we've ever had."

In Series 21 episode 1, the Stig's Teenage cousin appeared, with headphones on, a low waist line allowing his underwear to be seen and a phone he seldom stopped looking at. He drove a modern hot hatchback to set a hill run time against the presenter's classic hot hatchbacks.

The U.S. Top Gear, Top Gear Australia and Top Gear Russia also feature their own versions of The Stig. Top Gear Australia's Stig, when the UK-Australian "Top Gear Ashes" episode was filmed, was wheeled on, upside down in a delivery crate. Additionally, when Top Gear Australia visited New Zealand (in series 3 episode 2), they introduced their Stig's Kiwi cousin, "The Stug" (referencing New Zealand English's centralized short-"i" sound). When Top Gear U.S. drove a modified off-road racer through Colorado against a kayak, they introduced "Backwoods Stig," who wears a white racing overall with torn off sleeves. The Stig's are rarely used in the US version as presenter Tanner Foust is himself a professional racing driver.

In the DVD Top Gear: "The Worst Car in the History of the World", the Stig's Yorkshire cousin was featured. Alongside his trademark racing outfit, he had a flat cap on his helmet and two whippets by his feet. He was involved in driving a BMW around a Gymkhana course to show how it is done for when James and Jeremy attempt to do so with two of the worst American cars. He was also prompted in driving one of the worst cars that was the candidate for the title, but he fled.

Series One

And so the show we all know and love commences... Series 1 ...The new series of Top Gear takes up home at Dunsfold Aerodrome in Surrey. Dunsfold Aerodrome is a former Royal Canadian Air force base used during WII. It is now a working aerodrome, and features a purpose built test track which links with the aerodromes runways. The 1.75 mile track itself was built by Lotus Cars as a testing area purposely designed to put the vehicles under stress and test their understeer, cornering and braking capabilities. In the past the track has been used to test various Formula One cars as well as the development of a number of supercars including the McLaren 12C.

The first series of the relaunched Top Gear was broadcast in the United Kingdom on BBC Two starting on 20th October 2002, and concluding on 29 December 2002, and contained 10 episodes.

Episode	Reviews	Challenges	Star in a Reasonably Priced Car
1 20/10/2002	Citroën Berlingo Multispace• Pagani Zonda• Lamborghini Murciélago• Mazda	Speed camera challenge	Harry Enfield (2:01)
2 27/10/2002	Ford Focus RS • Noble M12 GTO	Bus jumping over bikes	Jay Kay (1:48)
3 03/11/2002	MiniOne• Toyota Yaris Verso • Citroën DS• Westfield XTR2 • Aston Martin DB7	Grannies doing doughnuts with a Honda S2000	Ross Kemp (1:54 Wet)

4 10/11/2002	Aston Martin Vanquish • Ferrari 575M Maranello • Nissan Skyline R34 GT-R	Family Saloon Formula One	Steve Coogan (1:53 wet)
5 17/11/2002	Mercedes-Benz S-Class • Audi A8 • Maybach 62 • Bentley Arnage	Create a Bond car	Jonathon Ross (1:57)
6 24/11/2002	Renault Vel Satis • BMW Z4 • Mercedes-Benz SL55 AMG • Honda NSX Type R	Grannies doing handbrake parking	Tara Palmer – Tomkinson (1:54 wet)
7 01/12/2002	Saab 9-3 • Lotus Elise 111SE	Fastest Faith (Part 1)	Ricky Parfitt(1:52)

8 08/12/2002	Audi RS6 • Mercedes-Benz E55 AMG • Maserati Coupé • Ford Fiesta • Citroën C3 • Honda Jazz • Nissan Micra • MG ZR • Lada Riva modified by Lotus	Fastest white van man	Sir Michael Gambon (1:55)
9 22/12/2002	Volvo XC90 • Subaru Forester • VW Golf R32 • Honda Civic Type R • Toyota Land Cruiser	Stripped down Jaguar XJS	Gordon Ramsey (1:50)
10 29/12/2002	Range Rover • Lotus Esprit • Nissan Primera • TVR T350C7	Fastest Faith (Part 2)	None today

Lamborghini Murciélago v. Pagani Zonda

In the first episode of new Top Gear, the Pagani Zonda is compared to the Lamborghini Murciélago. Jeremy drew similarities between the Zonda and an F15 fighter, "both have glass bubble roofs at the front & a lot of engine behind, and both have styled exhaust outlets." The noise from the Mercedes V12 with 555bhp and the lightness of the carbon fibre bodywork were both lauded, resulting in the Zonda's 220mph top speed. Jeremy switched to the Lamborghini Murciélago and sees what's what? As Audi now owns Lamborghini, Jeremy speaks of vastly increased drivability compared to Lamborghini's of old. Greater cabin space, a light clutch with smooth, easy gear changes, and a 6.2L V12 with 571bhp. The Murciélago is pitched against the Zonda in a drag race with the Zonda annihilating it. Pondering the loss, Jeremy claims the Murciélago is not so much a super car, but instead more like a great sports car, the best Lamborghini ever made and better than any current Ferrari, but not as good as the Zonda. The Zonda is crowned "The new king of super cars".

Maybach 62

Richard shows us the new Mercedes Maybach 62, at £281,380 its almost £200,000 more than the Mercedes S-Class Jeremy drove earlier in the same show. Richard took the Maybach to Germany. The soundproofing is so excessive, that even at 250kph the noise was minimal. Among other things, the Maybach features a photoelectric sunroof, which can be turned opaque at the touch of a button. Richard suggests the car looks a bit "sedate" for almost £300,000 worth of metal. Despite its size and weight, it can get to over 60mph in 5.4 seconds thanks in large to a 5.5L V12 with 550bhp and 900Nm of torque. Back in the studio, Jeremy tests out the boot auto-close feature by sticking his head in the opening. The closing boot lid detects his head and springs back up.

Noble M12 GTO

Jeremy introduces the Noble M12 GTO. A car built in Leicestershire with plastic panels and a Ford Mondeo engine. Jeremy admits this sounds rather poor, however says it's "not a bad car at all". Although the engine is from a Mondeo, in the M12 it has been fitted with two turbochargers – resulting in a 0-60mph time of 4.4 seconds and a top speed of 165mph. However the party piece is how the M12 goes around corners. Jeremy lauds the handling and out of all the cars he has ever driven, names the M12 as his favourite handling car. It turns out the Noble does have an extremely large turning circle, but this problem isn't enough to put Jeremy off it.

Westfield XTR-2

After episode 1 and the Zonda went around the track in a 1:23.00 time. Top Gear sent out a challenge to anyone who could supply a car that would lap faster than that. One of the responses came from a small company called Westfield, manufacturers of the XTR. Despite looking like a race car, it is actually road registerable. Jeremy has his doubts about it beating the Zonda (a car which has a 7.3L V12, compared to the XTR with a 1.3L motorcycle engine). While this may sound very underpowered, the XTR has no creature comforts, not even a windscreen in fact. All of this adds up to a kerb weight of 410kg, even a Mini weighs almost 3 times more. The engine is a 1300cc Suzuki Hayabusa with 170hp equating to a power to weight ratio of 460bhp/ton. The Zonda manages 440bhp/ton, suggesting the XTR may walk away with the prize. The Stig takes it for a lap around the track and returns a 1:22.60.

Nissan Skyline R34 GTR

Jason Dawe moves on to the Nissan Skyline range, cars he describes as "basically a huge PlayStation with an exhaust pipe on the back". When looking for a Skyline as a second hand buy, there's a bit to look out for. Jason outlines the history of the Skyline starting with the R32's racing successes. Jason introduces the R32, R33 & R34 before taking an R34 GTR for a drive. He praises the technology involved in the car and the fact it makes the car almost idiot proof. "The car kind of looks after you". Back in the studio, Jason suggests the R33 as the best buy – the older R32 being a bit long in the tooth and the R34 being still a bit expensive.

Honda NSX Type-R

Opening the sixth show, Hammond & Clarkson previewed the Honda NSX Type-R in the studio. Honda were trying to decide whether or not to sell the NSX in Britain. The Stig posts a time of 1:33.7 on a very wet track, faster than both the Ferrari 575 and the Noble featured in previous episodes. If you take the 4-second wet lap deduction, the NSX places neck in neck with the Lamborghini Murciélago. As with the Aston Martin featured in episode 4 of the series, the Stig also spun the Honda during one of his attempts at posting a time.

Series 2

Episode	Reviews	Challenges	Star in a Reasonably Priced Car
1 11/05/2003	Smart Roadster •Volkswagen Beetle Cabriolet• Bowler Wildcat• Bentley T2	Drag racer jet engine incinerates Nissan Sunny	Vinnie Jones (1:53
2 18/05/2003	Rolls-Royce Phantom • Rover P5 • BMW M3 • Audi S4	Fastest political party	Jamie Oliver (1:50)
3 25/05/2003	Volkswagen Touareg • Lexus SC430 • Hyundai Coupe • BMW Z8 • Perodua Kelisa	Country with the fastest supercar	David Soul (1:54)
4 01/06/2003	Jaguar R Coupe • Jaguar Mk II • Jaguar XKR-R • Aston Martin DB7 GT	How far can you drive until you become bored in a Mark 3 Jaguar XJR?	Boris Johnson (1:56)

5 08/06/2003	Porsche 911 Turbo • Ford Street Ka • Triumph TR6 • Renault Clio V6	Rally pit crew vs. women getting ready for a night out	Anne Robinson (1:57)
6 15/06/2003	Subaru Impreza WRX STI • Mitsubishi Lancer Evolution VIII • Vauxhall VX220 Turbo • Peugeot 206 GTI	Land speed record for caravan towing	Richard Whitely (2:06)
7 22/06/2003	Koenigsegg CC8S • Renault Mégane • Hummer H1 • Hummer H2	Crash Testing the Renault Megane with a real driver	Neil Morrissey (1:49)
8 06/07/2003	Nissan 350Z • Alfa Romeo 147 GTA • Citroën C3 Pluriel • Mercedes-Benz CLK500 Convertible • Audi A4 Cabriolet • Daihatsu Copen	The Race for the Universe	Jodie Kidd (1:48)

9 13/07/2003	Vandenbrink Carver • Volvo S60 R • GM HyWire	Drive Vauxhall Signum from the rear seat	Patrick Stewart (1:50)
10 20/07/2003	TVR 350C • Overfinch Range Rover • Cadillac Sixteen • Volkswagen Phaeton	Land Rover Reliability challenge	Alan Davies (1:54 wet)

Aston Martin DB7 GT

Jeremy moves on with the Jaguar XKRR, a lowered version of the XK with racing seats and seatbelts, racing tyres and uprated exhausts. While it may only be a concept car, it actually works. Jeremy takes it to the test track to see what's what. The XKRR has a manual gearbox and a limited slip differential, allowing the car to easily power slide, where the old XK would simply spin. While Jeremy loves the car, he explains Jaguar can't put it into production, due to Jaguar's sister company, Aston Martin. The XKRR would steal the limelight from the new Aston DB7 GT. Jeremy swaps cars and sees how it stacks up. The DB7 GT has a rather cramped interior, due to it actually being based on an old Jaguar XJS, a 13 year old car. The DB7 will set you back £104,000. Despite the aging chassis and old body shape, Jeremy says the DB7 is "amazing", going on to say all the little changes Aston made to the suspension has actually added up to make a big difference. The 6.0L V12 is also more powerful than the older model. Jeremy demonstrates this by stopping the car, then setting off in 4th gear from stand still without a judder. The DB7 can do 0 – 135mph in a single gear. Jeremy sums it all up, "For the last few years the DB7 has been an aging rocker, still trying to cut it in a Cold Play MP3 world of Porsche 911's and Foo Fighter Ferrari's. But now, thanks to a cocktail of botox and viagra it's up there with the best of them."

Renault Clio V6

Jeremy introduces us to the new Renault Clio V6 with a track test. The Clio has a 3.0L V6 mounted in the middle, where the rear seats would usually be. There's no room in the boot for shopping either. Jeremy goes on, "This is such a bloke's car! You start with a practical sensible family hatch back and then fill it full of engine. Who cares that you have to put the baby under the bonnet." The Clio V6 appears to be terribly impractical on all accounts and the list of equipment seems fairly basic for the £27,000 price tag. Jeremy rationalizes it all though, "This is as mid-engined as a super car, it sounds like a super car, it goes like a super car, so on that basis it becomes the bargain of the century. It'll do 155mph and out-accelerate the Porsche C4S we looked at earlier. I think it's fantastic." Jeremy's only doubt is that it'll still be savage once you exceed the limit of grip the Clio has, just like the older models. The Clio understeers as it gets close to the limit, then snaps into oversteer and even a spin once you exceed it. Jeremy suggests the problem is that "It's French, it's a surrender monkey. If you show it a difficult corner, it just sort of gives in… sits in a cloud of its own smoke with its hands up." The Stig takes the Clio V6 for a lap around the soaking wet track but manages a respectable 1.36.20 which was exactly the same time as an Aston Martin Vanquish in the same conditions.

Koenigsegg CC8S

Clarkson tested the Koenigsegg CC8S which, with a top speed of 242 mph (389 km/h) it was, at the time, the world's fastest production car. Clarkson did a speed run on the test track. The record of 170 mph (274 km/h) set by the Pagani Zonda was broken, with the Koenigsegg managing 174 mph (280 km/h). Clarkson later commented how he felt nervous before the run because engineers from Koenigsegg had asked him if they could put gaffer tape around the windscreen; he thought that the tape was to keep the windscreen from flying off. The Stig drives the Koenigsegg to a lap time of 1:23.9, which is just one-tenth of a second slower than the Zonda. Jeremy has frequently referred to the Ford Modular engine in the Ford Mustang as a "terrible engine" but declined to mention that the Koenigsegg's engine was a modified 4.6 L Modular V8.

Vauxhall VX220 Turbo

In the final segment, Jeremy power tests the new Vauxhall VX220 Turbo. The VX220 is based on the Lotus Elise, but Vauxhall have done their best to make it better by giving it a leather interior and extra sound proofing to make it more refined. Just like the Elise, Jeremy struggles to get into it, a job made easier by removing the roof first. The VX220 turbo produces only 200 bhp but Jeremy describes it as being "hugely fast" thanks to its light kerb weight. The 0-60 mph time is just 4 seconds and it keeps on pushing all the way up to 150 mph. Jeremy also thinks the VX220 handles better than the Elise, being a bit more "oversteery" rather than "understeery". He goes on to say "There's only one thing that's going to get me off this racetrack today, and that's when it runs out of fuel… and that's the first time I've ever thought that, while behind the wheel of a Vauxhall." Jeremy calls it the "Sportscar of the moment" before the Stig takes it for a lap returning a time of 1:31.30.

GM HY-Wire

James reviews the revolutionary GM Hywire, which runs on a mixture of hydrogen from the tank and oxygen from the air.

With the Hy-Wire and future prototypes, GM hope to reinvent the automobile.

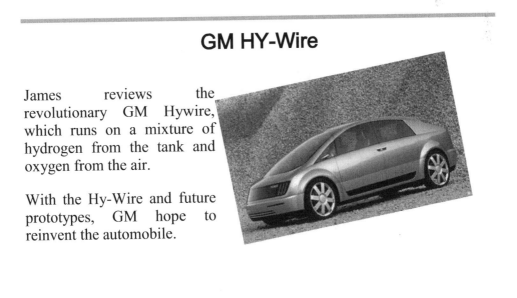

Cadillac Sixteen

James is the only one interested in the fate of Cadillac, so he sets out to see what they've done to reverse their market woes. He finds the astonishing 1,000 bhp (750 kW), naturally aspirated 13.6 litre V16 Cadillac Sixteen concept car. It shuts down cylinders to preserve fuel economy and has a badge carved from crystal in the center of the steering wheel. The interior is too cushy and the clock is too posh, but James loves it. Jeremy and James agree that this is the best Cadillac since 1966.

Series 3

The third series of Top Gear began on 26 October 2003, and concluded on 28 December 2003. The series featured 9 episodes. The series was subsequently followed by one "Best of Top Gear" special, charting the best moments from the series. The series was the first series of Top Gear to get more than 10 million viewers for an episode.

Episode	Reviews	Challenges	Star in a Reasonably Priced Car
1 26/10/2003	Ford GT • BMW 5-Series • Porsche 911 GT3	Can the diesel Volkswagen Lupo get better mpg than the petrol version?	Martin Kemp (1:54 wet)
2 02/11/2003	BMW M3 CSL • BMW M1 • BMW M3 • BMW M5 • Porsche Boxster • BMW Z4 • Honda S2000	Volvo 240 attempts to jump four caravans	Stephen Fry (1:54 moist)
3 09/11/2003	Bentley Continental GT • Subaru Legacy Outback	Saab 9-5 Aero versus a BAe Sea Harrier • How to Escape from a Sinking Car	Rob Brydon (1:48)

4 16/11/2003	Lamborghini Miura • Lamborghini Countach • Mini Cooper S Works • Lamborghini Gallardo	Lamborghini Tribute	Rich Hall (1:54) & Jay Kay (1:48)
5 23/11/2003	Mazda RX-8 • Fiat Panda	Is the Toyota Hilux really indestructible ? • Hammond searches for future classic cars	Simon Cowell (1:47)
6 07/12/2003	Citroën C2 • Aston Martin V8 Vantage (1977) • Holden Monaro	Is a Toyota Hilux really indestructible ? – Part 2	Sanjeev Bhaskar (1:51 wet)
7 14/12/2003	MG XPower SV • Porsche Cayenne Turbo • Mercedes-Benz SLR McLaren	Which professor can do the best burn-out? – What is the best British car?	Rory Bremner (1:47.9)

8 21/12/2003	Mercedes-Benz 280SL • Nissan Micra • Aston Martin Lagonda • Audi TT	Top Gear Generation Game	Johnny Vegas (1:58)
9 28/12/2003	Chrysler Crossfire • Smart Roadster (Brabus V6 Bi-Turbo) • Jaguar XJ6 • Honda Civic Type R • Honda NSX Type R	Top Gear Awards 2003	Carol Vorderman (1:51.2)

FORD GT

Jeremy travels to Detroit where he reviews the heavily-anticipated Ford GT. Jeremy relates his fond memories for the old 1960s Ford GT40 and looks at the GT against all its competitors. He reports that it handles like a Lotus Elise, goes faster than a Ferrari 360 Modena, sounds better than a Honda NSX, and shocks like a Lamborghini Murciélago. It is also considerably cheaper than the Ferrari and the Lamborghini with which it competes. For him it is a nostalgic evocation of 1960s Detroit and American muscle cars racing between the lights.

Bentley Continental GT

In the previous series all three presenters were clamoring for the chance to drive it, with it eventually being revealed that Jeremy won out. But he was not impressed. Though the car is good for overtaking (0-60 in 4.8 seconds) and it has an immensely high top speed of 198 mph (319 km/h), he found it to be too much of a Volkswagen and rather cramped inside. It seemed to lack character. Jeremy was forced to conclude it was a good car, but could never call it a great car.

Lamborghini Gallardo

Due to the 40th anniversary of Lamborghini, Hammond and May test some classic cars. Hammond tests the 1967 Lamborghini Miura, commenting on its controversial, trend-setting styling and engine positioning; and rides in an improved 1971 SV version with its owner, musician and supercar enthusiast, Jay Kay. May tests his childhood dream car, the Lamborghini Countach, finding it as fast and great-sounding as the bedroom posters suggested, but utterly terrible to drive, ride, and especially to park. Clarkson shows the Lamborghini LM002, a huge V12-engined SUV, and marvels at how much fuel it drinks and its comically poor handling. The modern Murciélago returns for a second power lap (after a wet lap in series 1), and proves the Black Stig's supposition that it would top the board with a dry track, setting a record time of 1:23.7.

Mercedes Benz SLR McLaren

Hammond reviews the Mercedes-Benz SLR McLaren in South Africa. He isn't impressed, especially by the brakes, hard ride, and interior quality. Back in the Top Gear studio, Richard and Jeremy engage in a game of Top Gear Top Trumps pitting Hammond's experience with the SLR McLaren against the Porsche Carrera GT, which Jeremy drove earlier in the year. They concluded that the Porsche is more the driver's car, but that you'll want the Mercedes if you are a golfer as your clubs will not fit in the Porsche.

Series 4

The fourth series of Top Gear began on 9 May 2004, and concluded on the 1st of August 2004. The series contained 10 episodes.

Episode	Reviews	Challenges	Star in a Reasonably Priced Car
1 09/05/2004	Lotus Exige • Rover CityRover • Aston Martin DB9	Epic race: Aston Martin DB9 vs. TGV and Eurostar French fast trains – London to Monte Carlo • Apache Gunship helicopter vs. Lotus Exige – can the helicopter get missile lock?	Fay Ripley (1:53 mildly moist)
2 16/05/2004	Mercedes-Benz SLR McLaren • Alfa Romeo 166 • Cadillac Escalade • Ford FAB-1	A nun in a monster truck • Hammond gets hypnotised	Paul McKenna (1:48)
3 23/05/2004	Porsche 911 GT3 RS • Ferrari 360 Challenge Stradale • 1968 Dodge Charger 440 R/T	£100 car challenge. (Volvo 760 V6 GLE, Audi 80, Rover 416GTi)	Jordan (Katie Price) (1:52)

4 30/05/2004	Porsche Carrera GT • Audi A8 TDi V8 • Ford SportKa	'Car darts' • V8 Diesel Audi A8 endurance challenge (London to Edinburgh and back on one tank) • Ford SportKa vs. racing pigeons • Evo vs. STi battle revised	Ronnie O'Sullivan (1:47.3)
5 06/06/2004	MG ZT 260 • BMW 645Ci • Jaguar XK-R • Porsche 911 Carrera 2 • Vauxhall Astra • Mazda3 • Volkswagen Golf	Shootout: Performance sport coupes on the Pendine Sands • Volkswagen Golf gets electrocuted	Johnny Vaughan • Denise van Outen (1:53.2)
6 13/06/2004	Renault Clio RenaultSport • Jaguar XJS • Cadillac CTS • Nissan Cube	Can you run a car on poo?	Sir Terry Wogan (2:04)
7 11/07/2004	Spyker C8 Spyder • Mercedes-Benz CL 65 AMG	MPVs as minicabs: (Renault Scénic • Ford C-Max)	Lionel Ritchie (1:50)

8 18/07/2004	Ford GT • Maserati Quattroporte	Diesel versus Petrol hot hatch race • Blowing over cars using Boeing 747 jetblast • Tribute to the Rover V8 engine	Martin Clunes (1:50)
9 25/07/2004	Fiat Barchetta • Mercedes-Benz SL600 • Mazda MX-5 • Toyota MR2 • Jaguar X-Type Estate	May and Hammond search for the best convertible roadster • Can you parachute into a moving car?	Sir Ranulph Fiennes (1:51)
10 01/08/2004	Volvo V50 • BMW X3 • Chevrolet Corvette	Hammond drives the Peugeot 407 as a pace car • Car Olympics: long jump	Patrick Kielty (1:48)

Aston Martin DB9

In a race to Monte Carlo Hammond and May take the Eurostar and TGV, while Clarkson drives the Aston Martin DB9. Clarkson admits that it would not be possible to beat the Eurostar and TGV in an ordinary car, but adds that the DB9 is no ordinary car. Hammond and May are not allowed to use any cars and Clarkson is not allowed to use any train. The finish line is the Café de Paris in Casino Square in Monte Carlo. Clarkson opens up a big lead in the DB9, but just over halfway through France, Hammond and May overtake him on the high-speed TGV. However, as the TGV line runs along the south coast, the train slows down as it approaches Monte Carlo and Hammond and May have to change trains. Clarkson accelerates the DB9 to speeds of over 120 mph and takes back the lead, arriving at the café about 2 minutes before Hammond and May. Clarkson calls the DB9 "motoring perfection" and consistently praises it over all of its competitors and its big brother the Vanquish.

Porsche 996 GT3 RS v. Ferrari 360 Challenge

Cars for track days, Porsche 996 GT3 RS versus Ferrari 360 Challenge Stradale. Both cars are heavily stripped down with minimal amenities. Clarkson remarks that the Porsche is very plain, while the Ferrari is very complex, and finds the Ferrari is the more astonishing track car. But because the performance is so similar, and the Porsche is so much cheaper, he recommends the Porsche if track times are the only concern. Both cars scored a Power Lap time of 1:22.3 in the hands of the Stig.

Porsche Carrera GT

Clarkson looks at the Porsche Carrera GT from a "German point of view", explaining its mechanics and silicon carbide with fascination and quiet innuendo, and then gives it a second look from a British standpoint, allowing himself to be overwhelmed by its sheer power. When run around the track (against the (automatic) Mercedes-Benz SLR McLaren time of 1:20.9 from episode 2), it beats the SLR by 1.1 seconds with a lap time of 1:19.8. Clarkson is taken by surprise by the car's qualities while comparing it to other German fast cars. It is unforgiving and highly-strung, unlike the GT-like SLR, and although normally Jeremy doesn't like the cold, clinical German supercar, he concludes that this one breaks through the stereotype to gain his full respect. However, as compared to the SLR, it is less powerful, much more difficult to drive, has no luggage space to speak of, and costs more.

Spyker C8 Spyder

A Spyker C8, which the Stig drives to a lap time of 1:27.3. It has a lot of power, but the chassis can't use it well. The styling is however praised as marvelous by Jeremy. It's designed "for those who want to look good at 4 mph rather than those who just want to go 400".

Series 5

The fifth series of Top Gear began in the United Kingdom on 24 October 2004 and concluded on 26 December 2004. The series contained 9 episodes.

Episode	Reviews	Challenges	Star in a Reasonably Priced Car
1 24/10/2004	Porsche 911 Carrera S • Vauxhall Monaro VX-R • Chrysler 300C • Jaguar S-Type R	Can an ice cream van jump a bouncy castle?	Bill Bailey (1:53.4)
2 31/10/2004	Ford Focus • Vauxhall Astra • Volkswagen Golf • Jaguar XJ220 • Pagani Zonda • Enzo Ferrari • Ferrari F40 • McLaren F1 • Porsche Carrera GT	Mountainboarder versus a rally car	Gerri Halliwell (1:55)
3 07/11/2004	Dodge Viper SRT-10	Drive a Land Rover Discovery to the top of Cnoc an Fhreiceadain in Scotland • Find the craziest car in the world • Top Gear	Joanna Lumley (1:51.5)

		survey 2004 results	
4 14/11/2004	Pagani Zonda S Roadster • Aston Martin Vanquish S • Ferrari 575M Maranello	24 hours in a Smart ForFour • Playing conkers with caravans.	Jimmy Carr (1:46.9) • Steve Coogan (1:53 wet)
5 21/11/2004	Morgan Aero 8 GTN • Mercedes-Benz 300SL	People carrier racing • Break 10:00 around the Nürburgring Nordschleife in a diesel car	Christian Slater (1:51.4)
6 05/12/2004	Volkswagen Golf V GTI	How much Porsche can you get for £1500? Porsche 924, Porsche 944, Porsche 928 • Blind man doing a power lap	Cliff Richard (1:50) • Billy Baxter (2:02)
7 12/12/2004	Toyota Prius • Ford Mustang • Mitsubishi Lancer Evolution VIII MR FQ400 vs a Lamborghini • Top Gear Awards 2004	A four-door Evo goes head-to-head with a Lamborghini. Top Gear Awards 2004	Roger Daltrey (1:49.6)

8 21/12/2004	Ferrari 612 Scaglietti	Epic race: Ferrari 612 Scaglietti vs Jet Plane to Verbier • Showroom cars vs old race cars • Mitsubishi Evo vs bobsleigh • Stig attempts a sub-1:00 power lap of the test track in a Renault F1 car	Eddie Izzard (1:52)
9 26/12/2004	Ariel Atom • BMW 1 Series • Mercedes-Benz G55 AMG	Find a 'pearl' among a collection of cars from the Pacific Rim	Trinny Woodall (1:54.1)• Susannah Constantine (1:55.7)

Jaguar XJ220

Clarkson compares two trios of supercars: three older supercars, the Jaguar XJ220, the McLaren F1 and the Ferrari F40, and three newer supercars, the Pagani Zonda, the Porsche Carrera GT and the Enzo Ferrari, coming to the conclusion that the simplicity of some of the older cars makes them more fun, even if they are slower around a track. Clarkson is very critical of the attitude of current supercar makers, claiming that they "held back" with cars like the Porsche Carrera GT, but is also critical of the McLaren F1, saying that driving it resembled trying to ride a nuclear missile á la Dr. Strangelove. As Jaguar's first production supercar, the XJ220 was a bold step for the British company. Looking at the company's history, you would have to stretch back to the XK120 to find an equally impressive machine. During the forty years between these models, there are many LeMans winning racecars and striking styling concepts, but nothing that pushes the same thresholds of performance while maintaining production readiness.

Aston Martin Vanquish S

The Aston Martin Vanquish S, which Clarkson tests in a race against Steve Coogan in a Ferrari 575M GTC. The Vanquish has been improved greatly, but it is still no match for the Ferrari on the track. However, as an all-rounder, with looks and comfort taken into consideration, Clarkson and Coogan would rather have the underdog Aston than the big-headed Ferrari.

Mercedes-Benz 300SL Gullwing

The Fender Stratocaster guitar and the Mercedes-Benz 300SL Gullwing both celebrate their 50th birthdays, so as a result, instead of talking about a restored car, May talks about the reasons why the Gullwing is the first supercar, with songs performed with the Stratocaster playing in the background including Voodoo Child (Slight Return), Sultans of Swing, China Girl, Layla, Get It On, and Wind Of Change (the single song in the set that is from Germany, as is the SL300 Gullwing).

Ferrari 612 Scaglietti

Hammond and May, using a plane, raced Clarkson who drove a Ferrari 612 Scaglietti from London to Verbier in Switzerland. It looked good for Hammond and May when they arrived at Geneva miles ahead of Jeremy, who was still in France. Clarkson had to stop a few times because his car developed a buzzing noise and he was stopped by the police. Despite this, he made up time while the others were waiting for trains and buses. Clarkson won again but only by minutes. He overtook the others on the road just a few hundred yards away from the finish line.

Series 6

The sixth series of Top Gear aired on 22 May 2005 and concluded on 7th of August 2005. A total of 11 episodes were broadcast, the most of any Top Gear series. It also began the "Some say..." introduction to the Stig.

Episode	Reviews	Challenges	Star in a Reasonably Priced Car
1 22/06/2005	Mercedes-Benz CLS55 AMG • Honda Element	Toyota Aygo Football • Range Rover Sport vs Challenger 2 Tank	James Nesbitt (1:51.3)
2 29/05/2005	Maserati MC12	2 door coupé for less than £1500 that isn't a Porsche (Mitsubishi Starion, Jaguar XJS, BMW 635CSi)	Jack Dee (1:53.5)
3 12/06/2005	Aston Martin DB9 Volante • Maserati Bora • Wiesmann MF 3 • TVR Tuscan	Clarkson opens a public pool with a Rolls- Royce	Christopher Eccleston (1:52.4)

4 19/06/2005	Cadillac CTS-V • Renault Modus • Honda Jazz • Peugeot 1007 • BMW 320d	Presenters' mums help evaluate cars. • Can a stretch limo jump over the wedding party?	Omid Djalili (1:51.5)
5 26/06/2005	Aston Martin DB5 • Jaguar E-Type • Nissan Murano • Maserati GranSport • Which one is best avoiding bullets?: (Porsche Boxster S vs Mercedes-Benz SLK 55 AMG)	Soldiers shoot at Clarkson while he drives the Porsche Boxster S and the Mercedes-Benz SLK 55 AMG to see which one is best avoiding bullets	Damon Hill (1:46.3)
6 03/07/2005	Aston Martin DBR9 • Mercedes-Benz SLR McLaren	Epic race to Oslo: Mercedes-Benz SLR McLaren vs. a boat	David Dimbleby (1:52)
7 10/07/2005	TVR Sagaris	Fiat Panda against a marathon runner • Sabine Schmitz attempts to beat 10:00 around the Nürburgring in a Ford Transit	Justin Hawkins (1:48)

8 17/07/2005	Ferrari F430 • Audi TT • Nissan 350Z • Chrysler Crossfire	Convertible versions of existing coupes in Iceland	Tim Rice (1:52.7)
9 24/07/2005	BMW M5 • Vauxhall Astra VXR • Renault Mégane Sport • Volkswagen Golf GTI	"Road Test Russian Roulette" • World record attempt for number of times a car has rolled at high speed	Chris Evans (1:47.9)
10 31/07/2005	BMW 535d • Bentley Continental Flying Spur	Driving over a lake in Iceland • What is the most fun off-road toy	Davina McCall (1:56.9 Very wet) Mark Webber (1:47.52 Very wet)
11 07/08/2005	Ford F150 SVT Lightning • Vauxhall Monaro VXR • Lamborghini Murciélago Roadster	Recreate Top Gear Theme Song using engine sounds.	Timothy Spall (1:51.1)

Mercedes-Benz CLS55 AMG

Clarkson tests the Mercedes-Benz CLS55 AMG, a stylish and comfortable four-door coupe with a throaty 500 bhp (370 kW) supercharged V8, brakes from the SLR supercar, a luxurious interior, and "fabulous handling." The Stig does a lap time of 1:26.9, currently the fastest four-door saloon ever tested. Jeremy adores it as a "thug in a silk dressing gown" and says the only thing that would keep him from buying one is fear of the recent reputation for dodgy Mercedes-Benz build quality.

Maserati MC12

After destroying the disappointing Maserati Biturbo and lauding the Maserati 250F for its performance in the hands of Juan Manuel Fangio in the 1957 German Grand Prix, Clarkson announces the £412,000 Maserati MC12, saying it is "An Enzo in Drag". He is impressed with its speed, but, like the Biturbo, doesn't consider it to be a proper Maserati.

Aston Martin DB5

Clarkson returns to the 1960s to define cool with the Aston Martin DB5 and a Jaguar E-type. In standard, antique form they are terrible to drive, unreliable, extremely expensive, and slower in a drag race than a 2.4 litre Honda Accord. But he also recommends that nearly all of these problems can be overcome by spending somewhat more money on a modernised and updated version. The Stig takes both of them around the track; the original DB5 is the slowest car ever at 1:46, while the modernised E-type sets the same time as a V6-engined Audi TT at 1:32.

Aston Martin DBR9

The Aston Martin DBR9 racer is given a race around the track. It sets a very quick time of 1:08.6, but can't go on the board because it is not a production vehicle & it was on slick tyres.

Lamborghini Murciélago Roadster

Hammond participated in the Pamplona Bull Run in Spain, where he was shoved into the path of a bull by a participant, before a segment in which he road tested the Lamborghini Murciélago Roadster.

.

Series 7

The seventh series of Top Gear began on 13 November 2005, and concluded on 27 December 2005. The series contained seven episodes, one of which being the Winter Olympics special.

Episode	Reviews	Challenges	Star in a Reasonably Priced Car
1 13/11/2005	Ascari KZ1 • Aston Martin V8 Vantage • BMW M6 • Porsche 911 Carrera S	Shootout: Performance sports coupes on the Isle of Man • Top Gear survey 2005 results	Trevor Eve (1:48.4)
2 20/11/2005	Porsche Cayman S • Audi RS4	Life-sized RC cars • History of British racing green • Audi RS4 vs Speed Climbers race	Ian Wright (1:47.8)
3 27/11/2005	Ford Focus ST	Supercar road trip to Millau Viaduct, France (Ferrari F430 Spider • Pagani Zonda S • Ford GT)	Stephen Ladyman (1:48.8)
4 4/12/2005	Pagani Zonda F	Italian mid-engine supercars for less than £10,000 • Renault Clio vs.	Dame Ellen MacArthur

		downhill cyclist race in Lisbon.	(1:46.7)
5 11/12/2005	Marcos TSO • Bugatti Veyron • Porsche 911 Carrera 4	Epic race: Bugatti Veyron versus Cessna 182 Private Plane from Alba, Italy to London • RWD vs. AWD Porsches debate: Porsche 911 Carrera 4)	Nigel Mansell (1:44.6)
6 27/12/2005	Volkswagen Golf R32 • BMW 130i • Mazda MX-5	Old generation vs. New generation car culture • Lap times from a video game vs. Real life in the Honda NSX • Mazda MX-5 vs. Greyhound race • Top Gear Awards 2005	David Walliams (1:50.7) Jimmy Carr (1:46.9)
7 12/02/2006	None	Top Gear Winter Olympics	None

Ascari KZ1

Richard Hammond addresses the fictitious complaints of viewers that want a mid-level supercar in the £235,000 bracket. The answer: the Ascari KZ1, a British supercar (although designed by a Dutchman with an engine from the BMW M5). The Stig then takes the car to a 1:20.7, below the Porsche Carrera GT.

Pagani Zonda F

Hammond reviews the heavily revised Pagani Zonda F, with a carbon fibre Body, magnesium wheels, carbon-ceramic brakes, and an improved structure. The improvements to the car leave him genuinely speechless, and help it garner the fastest power lap time of 1:18.4 by The Stig.

Top Gear Special " Winter Olympics"

The trio travel to Lillehammer in Norway to recreate Top Gear's own version of the Winter Olympics. The losers of each challenge having to eat golden, yellow snow. The end credits of the episode were edited to show Jeremy Clarkson as Björn Clarkson, Richard Hammond as Benny Hammond, James May as Agnetha May and The Stig as Anni-Frid Stig, whilst every other crew member in the credits had their first name replaced with Björn as reference to the members of Swedish pop group ABBA.

Vehicles used were:

- Volvo XC90

- Audi Q7

- Citroen C1

- Jaguar XK

- Land Rover Discovery

- Mitsubishi Lancer Evolution

- Suzuki Swift

- Mini

Events:

Biathlon

Clarkson raced a Volvo XC90 against May in an Audi Q7, cross-country, with 2 shooting rounds mid-course while every shot missed target gives 5 penalty seconds. May used a standard Biathlon .22 rifle, while Clarkson opted for a H&K MP5 Sub machine gun. Despite the increased firepower, Clarkson missed every target and felled a tree. May missed only 2 targets in the final shooting round. However, near the end, he crashed into a tree and had to dig himself out. Despite this, May re-overtook Clarkson at the end and won the race.

Cold Weather Endurance

Hammond was subjected to Arctic temperatures in a Citroen C1, in a bid to see who will crack first: man or machine? After being subjected to a temperature of about minus-40 Celsius, Hammond narrowly beat the car, concluding that 'if you're going to drive to the North Pole, buy a Hammond'.

Speed Skating

Clarkson raced a Jaguar XK against a human skater, introduced by May as Eskil Ervik, on the ice course of Vikingskipet Olympic Arena. Clarkson was terrible at this event as his Jag had no grip whatsoever, being lapped twice by Ervik.

Off-Road Slalom

May and Clarkson raced a 4x4 Land Rover Discovery and a two-wheel drive Jaguar XK against the clock, on just about five inches of frozen lake. May declared himself the winner as he was the fastest with 2:03.28, but was disputed by Clarkson, who claimed his run to have been more graceful and interesting.

Bobsleigh

In an attempt to avenge a previously failed attempt, Hammond and a bobsleigh team race against May and a Mitsubishi Lancer Evolution rally car piloted by Norwegian Henning Solberg, along near-identical courses. Hammond won with 59.68 in the end, May's time was 1:02.24.

Ice Hockey

Ten Suzuki Swift's played 5-a-side hockey, in teams captained by Hammond and May, and refereed by Clarkson. May's team was called "primetime television" playing in Buffalo Sabres colours, while Hammond's team was called "daytime television" playing in Montreal Canadians colours. At one point, Hammond's team were winning 3-0, but a biased Clarkson intervened and successfully helped May to 3-2. Hammond's team then scored two more goals. Later, Hammond crashed into May's car and was sent to the penalty box, so May could score another goal. The result was supposedly 5-4 to Hammond's team, although only three of May's team's goals were shown in the programme.

Ski Jump

The trio attempt to find out if a rocket-powered 1986 Mini could jump further than a skier from a downhill slope. The Mini didn't manage to beat the skier and ended up crashing into a wall of hay made at the end of the ski jump, but the fact that they did manage to get a car down a ski jump is extraordinary nonetheless. The challenge was then concluded by a ski jump on a snowmobile driven by The Stig after which Clarkson joked about the pain that The Stig would have been feeling on his landing.

Series 8

The eighth series of Top Gear began on the 7th of May and concluded on the 30th of July, 2006. The series featured eight episodes. A new opening title sequence was introduced which featured segments of footage from the previous series and silhouettes of the presenters (the sequence would be updated over time with footage from later series), while the programme was now presented from a new and much bigger studio, as the production had outgrown the old one. The new studio is at Dunsfold Park Aerodrome, which is still the same location as the old smaller studio. This series also saw "Top Gear dog" introduced, a 'labradoodle' who's terrified of cars, which makes her violently ill and she also seems to hate James May, having thrown up on him when she arrived at the studio earlier in the morning before filming of the first episode. Top Gear Dog was only featured in the eight series and never appeared in any future series.

Over 150 complaints were received regarding actions carried out in the sixth episode, ultimately resulting in a caravan being burnt. Clarkson later proclaimed that it was not an 'accident' as first implied, but a publicity stunt to show everyone how much Top Gear hate caravans

Episode	Reviews	Challenges	Star in a Reasonably Priced Car
1 07/05/2006	Koenigsegg CCX • Honda Civic • Nissan Micra C+C	The Convertible People Carrier	James Hewitt (1:47.69) • Alan Davies (1:50.3) • Trevor Eve (1:47.09)• Jimmy Carr (2:08.91)• Justin Hawkins

			(1:48.44)• Rick Wakeman (1:55.26) • Les Ferdinand (1:47.41)
2 14/05/2006	Chevrolet Corvette Z06 • Jaguar XK vs. Mercedes-Benz SL 350 vs. BMW 650i	Kayak race in Iceland • Presenting a drive time radio show, how hard can it be? • The Stig does a farewell lap for the Suzuki Liana	Gordon Ramsay (1:46.38)
3 21/05/2006	Lotus Exige S	Amphibious cars challenge	Philip Glenister (1:54.3 wet)
4 28/05/2006	BMW Z4 M vs. Porsche Boxster S • Koenigsegg CCX Top Gear Wing • Mercedes-Benz S500 • Porsche Cayenne TurboS	Designing "Anne Hathaway's Cottage" in a Mercedes S280 • Porsche Cayenne vs. parachutist	Ewan McGregor (1:48)
5	Prodrive P2 • Citroën C6	Car football game II • Time-trial challenge	Sir Michael

04/06/2006		with Sir Jackie Stewart	Gambon (1:50.3)
6 16/06/2006	Ford Mondeo ST220 vs. Mazda 6 MPS vs. Vauxhall Vectra VXR	Caravan holiday • Indoor speed record in an F1 racer	Brian Cox (2:01)
7 23/06/2006	Lamborghini Gallardo Spyder • Peugeot 207 1.6L Diesel • Ford S-Max 2.5L 200 PS • Mercedes-Benz B200 Turbo • Vauxhall Zafira VXR	Caterham Seven kit car race • Peugeot 207 vs. parkour masters race in Liverpool	Steve Coogan (1:50.9 hot)
8 30/06/2006	Noble M15 • Ford Transit vs. Renault Master vs. Volkswagen T30 TDI 174 Sportline	£1000 Van Man challenge (Ford Transit, LDV Convoy, Suzuki Super Carry) • Being van roadies with The Who	Jenson Button (1:44.7 hot) Ray Winstone (1:51.4 hot)

Koenigsegg CCX

Clarkson reviews the new £415,000 Koenigsegg CCX and claims it is his new way of giving up smoking. The old Koenigsegg CC8S, which he reviewed in Season 2, Episode 7, was a raw, unruly beast that he found exceptionally fast, but very difficult to drive. The new car is even more so. Power lap: 1:20.4. The Stig lost control of the car upon a second attempt to break the posted time and hit a tire wall. He suggested that with the addition of a rear wing (later dubbed 'Top Gear wing') to provide downforce, the CCX would be 4 seconds faster.

Lotus Exige S

Clarkson reviews a Lotus Exige S on the Top Gear test track. The impressive handling from its predecessor has been retained, but a supercharger has been added to the Toyota engine that will propel the Exige to 148 mph with a 0-60 time of 4 seconds. This makes the Exige S the fastest accelerating car Lotus has ever made. To illustrate this speed, Clarkson pits the Exige against a Ford Mustang driven by the Stig around the Top Gear Test Track short circuit. The Exige wins. Drawbacks include the price (£33,000), the road noise, and the awkwardness of getting in/out of the thing. The Stig turns in a Power Lap time of 1:25.1 (just ahead of the Lamborghini Gallardo).

Lamborghini Gallardo Spyder

Clarkson reviews the Lamborghini Gallardo Spyder. He spends the bulk of the review expressing his unbridled enthusiasm for the car. Having bought one himself, he comments that it is not the best driver's car in the world, but it is something that could be used every day. He sums up his review by stating, "It has the most important characteristic that I look for in a car... it's a laugh! ... I think it's absolutely tremendous!" The Stig set a lap time of 1:25.7.

Series 9

The ninth series of Top Gear began on the 28th of January 2007 and concluded on the 4th of March 2007. The series featured six episodes, with a further two specials ("Top Gear of the Pops" and "Top Gear: Polar Special"), broadcast afterwards. The series also included one "Best Of Top Gear" special, charting the best moments from Series 8 and 9. The series' production was delayed due to Hammond's accident in September 2006, and did not begin until the following month. Subsequently, the first episode of the series has never been repeated on TV owing to Hammond's near-death experience.

Episode	Reviews	Challenges	Star in a Reasonably Priced Car
1 28/01/2007	Jaguar XKR vs. Aston Martin V8 Vantage	Roadwork's in 24 hours • Richard Hammond's Vampire dragster crash aftermath	Jamie Oliver (1:47.7 v. wet)
2 04/02/2007	Audi TT vs. Mazda RX-8 vs. Alfa Romeo Brera	Bugatti Veyron to top speed at Ehra-Lessien • Shootout: Best looking cars that can be called art • The team plays golf.	Hugh Grant (1:47.7)

3 11/02/2007	None	US Special	None
4 18/02/2007	Brabus S Biturbo roadster (based on a Mercedes-Benz SL65 AMG) • Porsche 911 Turbo	Reliant Robin Space Shuttle challenge	Simon Pegg (1:48.5)
5 25/02/2007	Lamborghini Murciélago LP640	Railway crossing hazard video • Tractor challenge (Fendt 930 Vario, JCB Fastrac 8250, Case STX Steiger 530):• Top Gear survey 2006 results	Kristin Scott Thomas (1:54)
6 04/03/2007	Shelby Mustang GT500	Stretch limos from ordinary cars (Fiat Panda, MG F, Alfa Romeo 164 V6 & Saab 9000 V6)	Billie Piper (1:48.3)

7 04/03/2007	Shelby Mustang GT500	Stretch limos from ordinary cars (Fiat Panda, MG F, Alfa Romeo 164 V6 & Saab 9000 V6)	Billie Piper (1:48.3)
8 25/07/2007	None	Polar Special	None

Jaguar XKR

Jeremy reviews the Jaguar XKR against the Aston Martin V8 Vantage. Although the Aston is better in some parts (better looking, louder, more aggressive, higher pedigree), Clarkson notes that the Jaguar is able to keep up with the Aston around the Top Gear track. The Jag is also more powerful, better equipped, more practical, and less expensive than the Aston. As Clarkson puts it, "It is quite simply spectacular." The Stig turns in a Power Lap time of 1:34.7 in "very, very, very" wet conditions.

Bugatti Veyron

May takes the Bugatti Veyron to its top speed of 407 km/h (253 mph) on Volkswagen's Ehra-Lessien test track. He described how smoothly the car behaved at those speeds and how disorienting the speed can be. He remarked that as he was coming to a stop at the end of his run, he wanted to open the door, but "fortunately I looked at the speedometer and I was still doing 70."

Top Gear US Special

The trio point out the hassle of renting out a car, ranging from ignorant rental agents to not being able to find their car once it's pointed out to them. Their premise was to see if it could be cheaper to buy a car rather than rent so, as a result, on their trip to the United States, the three were given $1000 to find a used car. Clarkson bought a 1989 Chevrolet Camaro RS; Hammond a Dodge Ram 150 pick-up truck; and May a 1989 Cadillac Brougham that was the only car that had air conditioning. The trio had radios in their cars, so they pretended to be like truckers while communicating with the local truck drivers, and use codenames during their journey. Clarkson's codename was "Murderer," Hammond's was "Brokeback," and May's, being rather obvious, was "Captain."

The goal was then to get from Miami to New Orleans, with challenges along the way.

Challenge 1: (Fastest Race Track Lap): At the Moroso Motorsports Park, the 3 cars had to complete the track length in the quickest time possible. Though, with no Stig in America, they had to do with the Stig's American counterpart; a rather more obese version of the British original, dubbed Big Stig by the hosts. Clarkson's Camaro was quickest, and surprisingly May's Cadillac beat the pick-up truck.

Challenge 2: (0 mph-50 mph-0 mph): At a drag strip in the heart of Florida, they all had to reach 50 mph (80 km/h) and brake as soon as they got to the speed. Ahead of them was a river, with a selection of Alligators. The closest to the watery grave was, yet again, Hammond, for failing to look up when he reached 50 mph (80 km/h) and poor brakes.

Challenge 3: (Roadkill): Each presenter was given money to buy something for their car that would "make the journey more comfortable", Hammond bought a grill, Clarkson bought a shower to replace his air conditioning and May bought a shirt rack. They were then told that they would be camping that night and dinner was whatever they could find dead at the side of the road. Clarkson found an possum but May ran over it then found a tortoise but refused to run it over and set it back in a nearby swamp. Hammond found a squirrel which was collected and spent a while trying to figure out how he would "peel" it. As Hammond and May set up camp, Clarkson went to look for more roadkill, he came back with an enormous dead cow. May refused to eat it. During the night Clarkson and Hammond successfully destroyed the Cadillac's air conditioning.

Challenge 4: (Car decorating): The team had to decorate each other's cars with slogans which might lead to them getting shot at in Alabama. May painted pro-homosexual slogans on Hammond's car ("Man-love rules OK"), Hammond painted "Country and Western is Rubbish" on Clarkson's, and Clarkson painted "Hillary for President, "NASCAR sucks" and "I'm bi" on May's car. All three offended locals, and led to both the presenters and the crew members being chased out of town by friends of the owner of the State Line Pride gas station in Seminole, AL, who pelted the crew's vans with rocks, leading to a mad dash to wipe the paints off the cars.

Challenge 5: (Sell car): The team were originally going to sell the cars in New Orleans, and the winner would be whoever made the most profit. However, after seeing the damage caused by Hurricane Katrina, the team decided to give away the cars for free to a Christian mission. However, while Clarkson's and Hammond's were given away, James May was declared the loser as he was unable to find any claimants for his car. Also, a lawyer threatened to sue Clarkson for misrepresentation after she heard the car wasn't a 1991 Camaro (it was a 1989 model) and would drop the suit on payment of US$20,000.

Final results: Clarkson declared himself the winner and declared May the loser, although no points were given. They concluded that it was viable to buy, rather than rent, a car. Clarkson summed up the trip with his long-held opinion: "Don't go to America!"

Top Gear Polar Special

The Top Gear Polar Special project was coordinated by car manufacturer Toyota and Top Gear, with the help of 'Arctic Trucks', an Icelandic vehicle modification company. The vehicle used was a modified Toyota Hilux. Toyota promoted the event under the name "Hilux Arctic Challenge".

The idea was originally proposed by the BBC to coincide with the Polar Challenge race, an annual event where competitors race to the 1996 location of the magnetic north pole by trekking and cross-country skiing. The attempt would be shown as a one-off Top Gear special in 2007. As part of the challenge, the car would be racing against a dog sled, the traditional means of transport around the Arctic. James May and Jeremy Clarkson would drive the car, and Richard Hammond traveled with the dog sled, accompanied by driver Matty McNair.

The race began in 'Resolute', Canada's most northerly town.

Clarkson and May ultimately were the first to reach the finish in their Hilux, thus winning the race and achieving their goal of being the first to do so in a car.

Three vehicles were used for the challenge. Two 2006 Toyota Hilux double cab 3.0l diesel pickup trucks and one Toyota Land Cruiser 120, all heavily modified by Arctic Trucks. A trailer on 38" tyres was also used to carry part of the equipment and fuel ("A freeze-resistant mixture of diesel and AvGas", according to Jeremy). One Hilux was used by the presenters and was fitted with camera and sound recording equipment, the other two were used by the film crew, two driver/repair experts and one polar expert. All vehicles underwent the same extensive modifications to make them suitable for the Arctic conditions. The major modifications to the trucks included the standard wheels and tyres being replaced with bespoke Arctic Trucks wheels and 38" studded snow tyres. The tyres were able to run at pressures as low as 0.2 bar (3 psi) for better traction over snow. The wheel arches were raised and extended to protect (and accommodate) the larger tyres.

The standard 3.0-litre D-4D engine was modified to cope with the very low temperatures. Heaters were added to increase fuel and coolant temperature, a large heavy-duty battery was fitted and the air intake was modified. A 90 litre auxiliary fuel tank was also fitted, along with an extra-thick sump guard. The gearing ratio had to be lowered to 1:4.88.

Two winches that could be fitted either to the front or rear of each of the vehicles were carried, in case they got stuck in the snow.

The truck used by the film crew was later re-used by James May in his attempt to get close to the still-erupting Eyjafiallajokull volcano and bring back a souvenir. The vehicle was further modified to include a tyre cooling system which included environmentally friendly vodka instead of anti-freeze and a corrugated roof to prevent damage to the vehicle from ejected debris.

Work began on the vehicles in December 2006, at Resolute, Canada, from where the expedition would begin. Over 240 man-hours of labour were spent completely refitting the two vehicles in preparation for the journey. Testing of the vehicles began in February 2007, after which some further modifications were made to the vehicles — the suspension was altered and the original 29" tyres were replaced with 38" ones. Testing of the vehicles continued until April 2007 with repeated cold start evaluations being taken to make sure that the vehicles would start in all conditions. Meanwhile the presenters were sent to Austria to begin their cold weather training. This included learning how to erect a tent, build a makeshift aircraft runway, pull a sled and deal with polar bears. Also, Clarkson was pushed into the frigid water by their trainer, an SAS veteran. On 20 April 2007 the Top Gear presenters arrived in Resolute where they completed their training with a two-night expedition camping on sea ice. With help from satellite images provided by the BBC, the support team plotted the route that the expedition would take.

Polar explorer Sir Ranulph Fiennes was called in to speak with the presenters after their constant joking and horseplay during their cold weather training. As a former guest on the show who was familiar with their penchant for tomfoolery, Fiennes bluntly informed them of the grave dangers of polar expeditions, showing pictures of his own frostbite injuries and what remained of his left hand.

The expedition set out from Resolute at 1300 on 25 April 2007. The destination for this day was Bathurst Island, an uninhabited island where they would make camp. After leaving Bathurst Island, the team had to rely on satellite navigation to plan their route.

Travel on the first three days was fairly easy, as the ice was smooth and the expedition was able to make good speed. Things got more difficult on 28 April, however, as the terrain became more difficult to cross, with sharp-edged ice covered in thick snow making it difficult to obtain traction, as well as posing a danger to the tyres. At this point, the team were relying on their guides to scout ahead for a safe route, demolishing outcrops of ice with axes when necessary. The terrain became even more perilous further north, with the team having to cross a field of very thin ice. There was a real danger of the ice cracking and the car falling through due to the weight, so the vehicles had to be driven very slowly. At one point, Clarkson & May's vehicle became trapped when it fell partly through the ice, and had to be pulled free by an accompanying vehicle.

On the morning of 2 May 2007 the GPS system confirmed that the team had reached the 1996 location of the magnetic north pole at (or at least the reading showing on the GPS in the program, which is 0.7 miles SSE of it), making them the first people to reach within a mile of the magnetic north pole location of any year in a motor vehicle. From there, the Top Gear presenters were evacuated by plane, while the team drove on to the disused Isachsen weather station, where they made camp and checked the vehicles to make sure they were in good enough condition to make the return trip to Resolute.

Richard Hammond never made it to the pole, as it "seemed cruel to make him go the extra distance just so Clarkson could gloat".

Series 10

The tenth series of Top Gear was broadcast between 7 October 2007 and 23 December 2007, containing 10 episodes. It was claimed that between the filming of the ninth and tenth series, rival motoring magazine Fifth Gear broke into the Top Gear premises and burnt down the Cool Wall. However, it was later revealed that the incident was a publicity stunt dreamed up between old friends Clarkson and Vicki Butler-Henderson. The opening episode of the series mentions the incident.

Episode	Reviews	Challenges	Star in a Reasonably Priced Car
1 07/12/2007	Volkswagen Golf GTI W12	Road trip to find the greatest driving road in the world: Porsche 911 GT3 RS vs. Lamborghini Gallardo Superleggera vs. Aston Martin V8 Vantage N24	Dame Helen Mirren (1:52.8)
2 14/10/2007	Audi R8 vs. Porsche 911 Carrera S	Amphibious Cars Challenge II	Jools Holland (1:49.9)
3 28/10/2007	Ferrari 599 GTB Fiorano • Ferrari 275 GTS • Rolls-Royce Phantom	Bugatti Veyron vs Eurofighter Typhoon race • Peel P50 around	Ronnie Wood (1:49.4)

	Drophead Coupé	the BBC office • Lexus LS600 Auto-Parking System	
4 04/11/2007	None	Botswana Special	None
5 11/11/2007	Caparo T1 • Aston Martin V8 Vantage Roadster • Mercedes-Benz GL 500	London race	Simon Cowell (1:45.9)
6 18/11/2007	Honda Civic Type R	Mercedes-Benz E63 AMG Estate vs. BMW M5 Touring • Motorhome racing • Alfa Romeo 159 vs. tall man across the Humber estuary	Lawrence Dallaglio (1:47.4)
7 25/11/2007	Aston Martin DBS	£1200 British Leyland cheap-car challenge (Rover SD1, Triumph Dolomite Sprint, Austin Princess)	Jennifer Saunders (1:46.1)
8	Vauxhall VXR8	Renault R25 Formula One Car •	James Blunt

02/12/2007		Automobile history investigation • GPS satellite self-controlled BMW 330i	(1:48.3) Lewis Hamilton (1:44.7)
9 09/12/2007	Ascari A10	Britcar 24 Hour Endurance Race • Race: Fiat 500 vs. BMX riders through Budapest	Keith Allen (1:51.7 v. wet)
10 23/12/2007	German Performance Saloon cars: BMW M3 vs. Mercedes-Benz C63 AMG vs. Audi RS4 • Jaguar XF	Features Top Gear Awards 2007	David Tennant (1:48.8)

Best Driving Road in the World

The presenters each took a light-weight supercar to Mainland Europe to find the best driving road in the world. Clarkson drove a Lamborghini Gallardo Superleggera, Hammond a Porsche 911 GT3 RS and May an Aston Martin V8 Vantage N24. Clarkson's Lambo and Hammond's 911 were quick and civilised to drive, but May's stripped-out Aston race car intolerably hot and uncomfortable to drive. They ended up finding the "best driving road in the world" (from Davos to the Stelvio Pass). May admitted that his Aston was terrible; Hammond and Clarkson found their cars brilliant but could not recommend buying the lightened versions since the performance was not superior enough to justify the price jump.

Ferrari 599 GTB

Jeremy Clarkson reviews the Ferrari 599 GTB Fiorano, concluding that he respects its technology, but is not excited by it and would prefer a Ferrari 275 GTS. The Stig takes the 599 round the track in 1:21.22.

Top Gear Botswana

Special

The team are told to each buy a used car for up to £1500. Mocking the use of "Chelsea Tractors" for delivering children to school and driving up leafy lanes, rules for the challenge stipulate that the car purchased to cross the spine of Africa has to be two wheel drive, and not designed in any way for off-road use. Clarkson buys a 1981 Lancia Beta Coupe, May a 1985 Mercedes-Benz 230E and Hammond a 1963 Opel Kadett, which he nicknames "Oliver". Starting from the Botswana-Zimbabwe border, they must drive 1,000 miles (1,600 km) to the Namibian border. If at any time a presenter's car breaks down and cannot be restarted, he must complete the journey in a Volkswagen Beetle. While the Beetle turns out to be a suitable vehicle for such a challenge, the Beetle is the presenters' collective least favourite car of all time.

The trio then attempt to cross the Makgadikgadi Pan successfully. The first section of the Makgadikgadi salt pan has a thin solid crust, under which lies a mud like substance underneath. Almost immediately, May and Clarkson's cars begin to break through the crust. Desperate to shed weight, they strip down their cars to the basic shell, removing most of the interior trim and most of the panels. Hammond's car is light enough to cross the salt pan shedding only his spare tyre and radiator grill. Clarkson's car breaks down frequently, seemingly with electrical issues. For day two on the salt pans, dust becomes the problem, rather than the "gunk" underneath the salt crust. May and Clarkson cover their faces and re-dress to avoid choking on the dust, as each driver was now open to the elements due to having a bare shell. Hammond does not have to take such measures as he did not drastically modify his car earlier.

Shortly before beginning their trip onto the Makgadikgadi Pan, the Top Gear trio informally encountered Botswana's Vice President, Seretse Ian Khama, who displayed no qualms regarding the trio's journey across the flats. However, he did seem taken aback by the fact that the trio were attempting this in their old, used, two-wheel drive cars.

The team are given their next challenge… Time trials around a rally course by "The Stig's African cousin". Oliver achieves a time of 1:12 before being beaten by May's Mercedes-Benz with a 1:06. Clarkson's car however, fails to start, so The Stig walks away.

The following challenge is to cross the Okavango Delta; the presenters are told to make their cars "wild animal proof". May is able to replace several Mercedes-Benz parts, due to the car's popularity in Africa. Clarkson however cannot find any spare parts for his Lancia Beta so he jury-rigs new doors from soft drink cans, wood and corrugated iron, and attaches a megaphone. May paints "All Adders Are Puffs" on Oliver, and "Lite Bite Cafe" on Clarkson's Lancia Beta. At the same time, Clarkson and Hammond hide a cowbell as well as several cuts of meat (including a cow's

head) inside May's car, to attract wildlife.

The final result? Both Hammond and May made it to the border before Clarkson, who had suffered two more breakdowns during the final run. Although Hammond's Opel had survived relatively intact (the only major repair being the car's electricals), and May's car had hardly broken down at all, both Clarkson and May, to Hammond's horror, declared the winner to be the Volkswagen Beetle, which had completed the trip with no documented mishaps at all.

Series 11

The eleventh series of Top Gear was broadcast between 22nd of June 2008 until the 27th of July 2008. The series consists of six episodes. This series included a revised title sequence, following the same visual style as with the sequence used for Series 8 through 10, but incorporating footage from the two prior series. A new character (Top Gear Stunt Man) was introduced in the first episode of the series. Also for the first five episodes of this series, the "Star in a Reasonably Priced Car" becomes "Stars in a Reasonably Priced Car", featuring two celebrity guests every week, each one setting an individual laptime. In May 2008, after series producer Andy Wilman held a brainstorming session with the presenters and other production staff, various facts about the upcoming series were released. Wilman confirmed that series 11 would see the presenters, Clarkson, Hammond and May, gain more control over the flow of the show's popular news segment. The series included running jokes appearing in each episode: Clarkson showing an image he claims to have found on "the Internet" which is censored for the television broadcast; and, in the news section, May appearing to feign enthusiasm whilst presenting a brief news item about the Dacia Sandero with no further discussion before they move on to the next item.

Episode	Reviews	Challenges	Star in a Reasonably Priced Car
1 22/06/2008	Ferrari 430 Scuderia	£1000 Police Car Challenge• TG Stuntman: Austin Allegro jump in reverse world record • Investigating fuel economy: 5 supercars vs BMW M3 vs Prius	Alan Carr (2:08.9) Justin Lee Collins (1:51.8)

2 29/06/2008	Mitsubishi Lancer Evolution X • Subaru Impreza WRX STI	Race: Audi RS6 vs French Skiers • Mercedes-Benz CLK63 AMG Black Series • TG Stuntman: MG Maestro Cork-screw Jump	Rupert Penry-Jones (1:48.1) Peter Firth (1:47.1)
3 06/07/2008	Bentley Brooklands	Cheap Car Challenge: Alfa Romeos for £1000 (Alfa Romeo 75 V6, Alfa Romeo GTV 2.0, Alfa Romeo Spider)	James Corden (1:53.4 wet) Rob Brydon (1:51.7 wet)
4 13/07/2008	Alfa Romeo 8C Competizione	Epic race: Nissan GT-R vs Japanese Bullet Train	Fiona Bruce (1:57.4 very wet) Kate Silverton (1:54.7 very wet)
5 20/07/2008	Nissan GT-R	Classic luxury limousines: Mercedes-Benz 600 vs Rolls-	Peter Jones (1:46.9)

		Royce Corniche • Daihatsu Terios fox hunting challenge	Theo Paphitis (1:48.5)
6 27/07/2008	Gumpert Apollo • Mitsuoka Orochi • Mitsuoka Galue III	Showdown: The British (Top Gear) vs. The Germans (D Motor)	Jay Kay (1:45.81)

Ferrari 430 Scudereria

Jeremy has a question – "What's wrong with Ferrari?" He explains that Ferrari's seem to be built around technology rather than being built on passion and excitement. That's where the 430 Scuderia comes in. Jeremy says that manufacturers like Porsche and Lamborghini go to great lengths to hide what has been removed in order to lighten their track cars. Ferrari on the other hand, ignored that with their track version of the 430 and has let it all hang out. As a result, the car is 100kg lighter, but all of the usual comforts are gone, no satellite navigation, no stereo and the carpet has been removed exposing all of the welds in the body. Most people would then assume that with less comforts and gadgets, the Scuderia would be cheaper than your average 430, but you'd be wrong. The Scuderia is in fact £43,000 more expensive, carrying a price tag of £172,000. Despite the lack of gadgets and luxuries, the Scuderia does come with a few upgrades, silicon brakes, a new differential and a computer upgrade to the gearbox that allows the car to change gear in less than 60 milliseconds. The most notable difference however is a small switch on the steering wheel that allows the driver to turn the traction control and stability management down or off. The Scuderia is capable of doing 0-60mph in 3.5 seconds with a top speed of close to 200mph, thanks largely to the weight saving and a power increase totaling 510hp. Co-designed by Michael Schumacher, Ferrari claim that the Scuderia is actually faster around the Ferrari Test Track than an Enzo. Jeremy explains that it is a difficult car to drive fast though, referring to it as a street brawler, "Feels like it wants to Goose your Mother, vomit in one of your flower beds, go to the pub, get drunk and kick someone's head in". Happy in the knowledge that the Scuderia is indeed a proper Ferrari, the car is taken for a lap of the track, posting a time of 1:19.7.

Mercedes-Benz CLK63 AMG Black Series

Clarkson drives the Mercedes-Benz CLK63 AMG Black Series. The Black Series provides more power than the 481 horsepower (359 kW) standard. It is lightened and tightened and is the first car that Jeremy ever receives which comes with a warning from the manufacturer itself. However, it retains comfort, luxuries, an automatic gearbox, and civility. Clarkson goes driving just for the sake of driving, and finds it to be ideal from a purist's perspective. Clarkson calls it a perfect blend of supercar fun and practicality, and he calls it his new favourite car. According to Clarkson, the Stig also notes that it's the most fun car he had driven in years.

Nissan GT-R

Clarkson, reviews the Nissan GT-R and tests its abilities on the Fuji Speedway. He is impressed by its electronically-assisted handling and sheer attention to detail put into preparing each hand-crafted car to both provide and cope with the severe cornering, but is himself forced to stop when the strong G-forces cause him a strained neck, and he leaves the scene in an ambulance. The Stig, with a "weapons-grade titanium neck", survives driving the since-imported car to post a time of 1:19.7.

Series 12

The twelfth series of Top Gear contained eight episodes, and started airing on 2 November 2008, with the usual presenting team of Jeremy Clarkson, Richard Hammond, James May and The Stig. Clarkson was injured while filming the series, after crashing a lorry through a brick wall at 56 mph in the first episode's HGV challenge. The running joke regarding the Dacia Sandero continues from series 11, with the alteration that Clarkson is now the one making the announcement with feigned enthusiasm, to utter indifference from May (instead of vice versa). Each news segment also features one of the hosts wearing something unusual, like slippers or a garishly patterned shirt. The only reference to this is that one of the other hosts will, at some point in the segment, ask if they're wearing it for a bet. The Stig, instead of listening to music during power laps, now listens to Morse code. The final episode, the "Top Gear: Vietnam Special", aired two weeks after the rest of the series as part of the BBC's Christmas line-up.

Episode	Reviews	Challenges	Star in a Reasonably Priced Car
1 02/11/2008	Porsche 911 GT2 • Lamborghini Gallardo LP560-4	£5,000 Lorry challenge (Scania P94D, Renault Magnum, ERF EC11)	Michael Parkinson (1:49.4)
2 09/11/2008	Abarth 500 Essesse	Muscle Car Challenge: (Dodge Challenger SRT8 • Chevrolet Corvette ZR1 • Cadillac CTS-V)	Will Young (1:48.9 damp)

3 16/11/2008	Toyota i-REAL • Renault Avantime	Tuning challenge: Mitsubishi Lancer Evolution X? • Finnish folk racing • Corvette V-8 engine blender-made smoothie	Mark Wahlberg (1:48.7)
4 23/11/2008	Pagani Zonda Roadster F • Bugatti Veyron	Economy race from Basel to Blackpool Illuminations	Harry Enfield (1:49.7)
5 30/11/2008	Lexus IS F • BMW M3	Portofino to Saint- Tropez Race: Powerboat vs. Ferrari Daytona • Best bus for British city streets	Kevin McCloud (1:45.87)
6 07/12/2008	Veritas RS III • Caterham Seven Superlight R500	Did the communists make a good car? • Ford Fiesta with the Royal Marines	Boris Johnson (1:57.4 very wet)
7	Tesla Roadster • Honda FCX	50 years of British Touring Car racing • TG Stuntman takes	Sir Tom Jones

14/12/2008	Clarity	on Fifth Gear's caravan jump record • Top Gear Awards 2008	(1:52.2)
8 28/12/2008	None	Vietnam Special	None

The Best Truck

Challenge

The team were set a task. The producers gave them each £5,000 to buy the best truck they could find and then meet up at the test track for a series of challenges. The trucks arrived and Jeremy was eager to establish who bought what. James went first, introducing his Scania P94D, Jeremy went over his Renault Magnum, and Richard proudly displayed his ERF EC11. The first challenge was then handed to them... They were told to decorate their trucks and meet at Top Gear's secret alpine test track located in Bedfordshire. Shortly after arriving in their freshly redecorated Lorries, they were issued the second challenge of the day. They were each told to demonstrate their lorry driving skills by power sliding their trucks around the skid-pan. The Stig's lorry driving cousin (Rig Stig) was on hand to demonstrate just how it was done. The boy's attempt to do the same in their Lorries didn't go as planned, with Jeremy injuring himself in the process. The challenge continues and the boy's have received their next task. The Lorries lined up to enter the 2 mile long high speed bowl to see who had the fastest rig. Jeremy's Magnum managed 80mph, James in the Scania made a dismal 64.6mph and Hammond continued on to nearly 90mph. Next, each lorry would be required to perform a hill start. As an added incentive, each person would have an item of value placed behind their trailers to force them to not roll backwards during the hill start. Jeremy was up first with his beloved drum kit placed only a few feet behind his lorry. His hill start went perfectly, however James and Richard obviously thought it shouldn't have gone so well, destroying the drum kit and blaming it on Clarkson's driving. Hammond was up next, and as payback for his drum kit being smashed, Jeremy had brought along Hammond's Opel Cadet affectionately known as 'Oliver'. Needless to say, Hammond was rather un-impressed and backed out of the challenge after discovering his lorry could simply not pull the added weight of the trailer up the hill. James was the last to go, with Richard and Jeremy placing his prized grand piano by the back doors of the trailer. The hill start didn't go so well, with his grand piano ending upside down at the bottom of the hill.

Back at the Top Gear test track and the boy's had to endure one final challenge to test the speed, braking and toughness of their chosen Lorries. Each of them must accelerate to 56mph, drive through an obstacle and stop as quickly as possible. Hammond was first up, driving through the Top Gear Production Office and stopping in a very respectable distance. James was up next, picking up speed and ploughing through 600 filled office water cooler bottles before coming to a stop 40ft further down the track than Richard did. Jeremy's turn and all that stood between him and a year's supply of pies was a solid brick wall. The impact was enormous, injuring Jeremy's neck and ankle in the process. Back to the studio and Jeremy concludes that the Scania P94D was the better truck for the challenge.

The Renault Magnum was produced by the French Manufacturer Renault Vehicules Industriels and later Renault Trucks (also part of Renault, now Volvo) from 1990 to 2013. The Magnum was available in semi and rigid configurations, both configurations could be bought with a 6×2 or 4×2 drivetrain. The 6×4 is merely designed for heavy haulage uses.

Ferrari Daytona

To celebrate the 40th Birthday of the Ferrari Daytona, Richard heads to Portofino in Italy to take one for a drive in its native environment, the Italian Riviera. Richard's drive will take him from Portofino, along the coast to Saint-Tropez and despite its age, Hammond still thinks that the Ferrari Daytona is the perfect machine for the job, and rightly so, who wouldn't want to drive a car with a 4.4L V12? James, on the other hand, thinks that a boat would be a better way of getting from Portofino to Saint-Tropez and introduces the XSR 48, the world's fastest diesel production boat. The two decide to have themselves a little race, but before setting off, James can't help himself and boasts that Richard's Daytona, worth £200,000, is nothing compared to his £1,250,000 XSR.

The race starts at a very slow pace, with James limited to a speed of 3 knots (3mph), and Richard unable to use second gear, having to go straight from first to third gear to avoid damaging the gearbox before it reaches operating temperature. James takes the opportunity to explain that his route was 40 miles less than the 215 mile route Hammond had chosen, though Hammond was confident that he would maintain a higher average speed. He also explained that because the XSR is a fair bit of kit, it was required that he have an experienced co-pilot to control the throttle and trim. Steering and navigation would all be up to James, neither of which are his strong points.

Richard gives us a little more information on the Daytona, saying that back in 1968 when it was first released, it was selling for £10,000, making it the most expensive Ferrari at the time. However, only a year prior to its release, Lamborghini had just started selling the Miura, which was mid-engined and equally as stylish as any Ferrari on the market. As a result, the Daytona was labelled a "dinosaur" for having the engine in the front. The Daytona did have a major advantage over the Miura though, in that with the engine sitting at the front, the weight gave it more stability at top speed, 174mph in fact, whereas the Miura couldn't get close because the front of the car would become very light and unstable at high speed.

The speed of both Richard and James eventually increased, though James was quick to run into rougher seas and the ride was beginning to be very uncomfortable despite the suspension equipped seats. After a few too many hard knocks, the cabin camera inside the XSR gives way and loses some of its colour. James too was hurt and was in a bit of pain as the co-pilot reduced the speed back to 25 knots, allowing Richard to get a decent lead. Further along in the race, Richard and the camera crew got pulled over by the police. The police weren't convinced that Top Gear actually had rightful possession of the Ferrari and Hammond was unable to produce the correct papers, nor was he able to 'sort out' the situation like he thought he could, instead being told to follow them to the nearest police station. Unfortunately for James, he too was soon halted by the local authorities and asked to produce documents.

Both Richard and James were eventually given the all clear and the race resumed. James was released sooner than Hammond and managed to close the gap caused by the rough seas earlier. Richard was the first to arrive in Saint-Tropez, though the traffic held him up for too long and James grabbed the win. Richard arrived at the chosen finish line moments later, but was still convinced that the Daytona was the perfect machine for the job. James had no argument against that and pleaded for Hammond to let him drive the Ferrari back.

Top Gear Vietnam Special

The boys begin by explaining their next big adventure. They were to meet 6,000 miles away, in Saigan, the capital city of Vietnam. Upon arriving, Jeremy, Richard and James were each given 15 million Dong (₫15,000,000) to buy a set of wheels. After voicing their excitement at receiving a shoebox full of cash each, James made his way to the Fiat dealership and was shocked when he was told that his ₫15,000,000 was in fact the equivalent of only $1,000 US, and that a standard, bottom of the line Fiat 500 costs a whopping ₫560,000,000. James was again disappointed when even the local back street car dealers turned his money down. Jeremy had also discovered that his money was in fact, very little, and had resorted to begging people on the street to sell their car to him without much luck. Richard caught on quickly and had simply given up, retiring early to go to lunch instead.

Over lunch they discussed their dilemma. Clarkson made a valid point when he blamed the high prices on the fact that cars have not been in Vietnam for many years and had not been given enough time to depreciate in value. Richard also chimed in and pointed out that there were no "bangers" for sale either. May and Hammond, being the motorcycling enthusiasts they are, took notice of the amount of motorbikes around them and raised the idea of buying cheap scooters instead. Needless to say, Clarkson wasn't very impressed, but was convinced none the less. Hours later, the guys arranged to meet at the American War Museum to show off their newly acquired motorbikes. Richard was the first to introduce his Russian made Minsk 125cc trial bike, describing it as "the AK47 of bikes". James had got himself a Honda 50cc Super Cub, describing his purchase as the "greatest motorcycle in history". Jeremy, with a distinct lack of enthusiasm, introduced his Piaggio Vespa step through scooter.

The main challenge was then given to the boys. "You'll now attempt to achieve in 8 days what the Americans failed to achieve in 10 years. Get from the South of Vietnam, to the North. You will ride from here in Saigon, to Hạ Long City near the Chinese border, which is 1,000 miles away". James and Richard were ecstatic and were eager to get going, Jeremy shared his disgust and said that he couldn't even ride a motorbike. While expressing his disgust, we're shown what the traffic conditions are like and a chilling statistic is given. Vietnam experiences 4 times more road deaths each year, than Britain.

They were quick to find their next obstacle, Hammond, being vertically challenged, managed to find a helmet that fitted with no problems. Jeremy and James didn't have as much luck and had to get helmets custom built. Unfortunately, due to the lack of time, they had to employ a back street metal work to fabricate some helmets for them overnight, with amusing results. James ended up with a wok for a helmet, and Jeremy was given a bucket with chin straps. Ever so safety conscious or perhaps just nervous about his lack of experience on a motorcycle, Jeremy had attached several mirrors to the front of his scooter so he didn't have to turn his head as often. Ready to go, the boys lined up and counted down ready to set off and start the journey. When the countdown reached zero, James and Richard quickly took off, leaving Clarkson behind trying to work out how to even start his scooter. Richard and James steamed ahead, thought it wasn't long before James had his first problem for the challenge, his helmet was too awkward and he had to get rid of the wok, leaving just a colander to protect his head.

Clarkson eventually got going, thanks to some passersby, and also managed to trade his bucket helmet in for a proper helmet. He eventually caught up with the other guys during a brief stop and quickly set about finding the cause of his scooter feeling so out of sorts. They discovered that the rear wheel, whilst being held on very tightly, was still extremely wobbly. The driveshaft was so badly worn, the entire engine had to be replaced, the front brakes were also tightened, so that they worked at all, and to top it all off, James and Richard had left him behind again. Once more, Richard and James steamed ahead, and despite getting his scooter back on the road, Jeremy was soon on the side of the road with more mechanical troubles.

Darkness had fallen, and Richard was poking fun at James for the lack of speed his bike had. Getting closer to Đà Lạt, the hills were getting steeper and James was struggling until his bike eventually stopped altogether. Behind James, Jeremy was back on his bike, but disgruntled by the way his additional mirrors were reflecting his headlight back into his own face. Richard was the first to arrive in Đà Lạt, with James arriving shortly after, despite having to resort to pushing his bike. Many beers later, Jeremy finally arrived and was eager to eat, ordering snake soup with a side of snake salad. Hammond wasn't very much a fan of snakes, nor was he a fan of the still beating snake hearts that Clarkson and May were shoving in his face. Later on, after many shots of vodka, Jeremy and James snuck out to the bikes and flattened Hammond's helmet, and then in the morning, offered a bright pink helmet to replace it.

The next leg of their journey would see them travel to Nha Trang, 130 miles North East of Đà Lạt. Jeremy's already unbearable attitude towards the decision to take motorcycles was doubled when the weather turned nasty and the rain came down. Jeremy's headlight was the first casualty of the wet weather, followed closely by Hammond who was having difficulty keeping his engine running at all. James wasn't to be counted out of the bad luck either, running out of fuel whilst Richard and Jeremy managed to get their motorcycles back on the road. James was eventually saved by a nice gentleman on an old Russian motorcycle, who pulled over to donate some of his fuel. James was rather impressed by the generosity of the man and even offered him money, referring to it as "soggy Dong".

Jeremy and Richard didn't get too much further up the road however and had pulled in to a fuelling station to mend Hammond's broken clutch cable. A little while later and James arrived to hear some bad news from Jeremy. The producers had gotten so fed up with the boys replacing parts so often, that if their bikes broke down again and required more than just tools to fix, they would be provided with suitable backup transport, which was in the shape of a small motorcycle painted in the American stars and stripes and equipped with a speaker playing 'Born in the USA'. Knowing that being seen on a bike like that in Vietnam was surely a death sentence, the boys set off once more with a bucket load of extra determination.

In a rather strange turn of events, Clarkson was actually beginning to enjoy himself, or more so, Vietnam itself. James on the other hand, was struggling. Third gear on his bike was a rather tall one and his bike no longer had the power to keep up the speed necessary to stay in the gear long enough before coughing and spluttering. Despite the issues, the boys were together again for the first time since they left Saigon and when thunder storms set in, the boys were treated to a dazzling light show as the lightning struck off in the distance. Jeremy's headlight finally gave up for good and once again they pulled over, fearful of the American bike, to strap a torch to the front mudguard. Despite the intense traffic and the weather, they eventually made it into Nha Trang, safe and sound. Clarkson cheered himself up by buying Hammond a present, which in typical Clarkson fashion was thoughtful, yet completely and utterly impractical. He'd bought Richard a model sail ship, which just so happened to be as big as his motorbike.

After another nights rest and with the model Galleon strapped to the back of his bike, Hammond set off again with James and Jeremy. After many uncomfortable miles in humid weather, their next stop would be to get some new clothes in the town of Hội An. Upon entering a local clothing store, Jeremy pointed out that whilst Hammond would be able to find clothes his size, both he and James would have issues, requiring them to have clothes made especially for them. Lucky for them, the price for a tailor made suit was the equivalent of only £70. Upon discovering the price, and that it would only take a day to complete a tailor made suit, the boys began looking around for what material they could use and put their orders in. Richard, as fashionable as he is, didn't stop there however, and went and ordered himself custom made shoes to go with his new suit.

While they waited for their suits to be finished, James and Richard suggested taking their bikes to the beach, which resulted in a few minor thrills and spills on Jeremy's behalf. Clarkson eventually gave up and went and had a relaxing drink. May and Hammond continued on the beach and competed to see who could get closest to the water, a decision both would regret as their bikes got wet and refused to run. With Clarkson having a foot massage and James still trying to get his bike out of the water, Hammond stopped to talk with one of the locals, who worked around the language barrier by writing in the sand. He described to Hammond, that he was on this very beach in 1968 when American B52 bombers flew overhead, delivering a devastating payload which resulted in the loss of many lives, an unfortunate, but common sight during the Vietnam war.

Night fell and Hammond was still having trouble getting his bike to run. After taunting him a little, Clarkson and May decided to head in to town for something to eat, getting distracted along the way by hundreds of candles floating on a river in the centre of Hội An. In the morning, the boys got dressed in their new and very colourful suits and headed for the ancient capital of Huế. Richard did manage to get his bike going and much to Jeremy's dismay, caught up once again. James continued to struggle with speed and eventually fell behind once more. Clarkson thought of it as the perfect opportunity to buy James a present. With the help of Richard, Jeremy once again bought another present that was thoughtful, but an absolute nightmare when it came to carrying it on the back of a motorcycle. When May arrived, Jeremy and Richard proved that despite the awkward size and weight of the statue, they had actually put a lot of thought into buying the right one.

After strapping the statue to the back of May's bike, they were back on the road again. May was being even more cautious than usual to keep his statue in tact, whilst Hammond had obviously forgotten about the size of the ship he was carrying and broke all of the masts off when he clipped some rubbish bins on the side of the road. Further down the road, he also managed to take out a traffic sign when passing through a toll booth. Moments later, Jeremy's bike came to a stop, claiming it "came over all Italian again". Wedging a plastic bag filled with weeds in with the electrical wires kept them from shaking about and the Vespa was alive again.

Full of confidence once again, the boys tackled a road the winded its way up a tall mountain and in the process, found an absolute cracker of a road that Jeremy labelled as a "deserted ribbon of perfection, one of the best coast roads, in the world". Backed by Jimi Hendrix's, Voodoo Child, the boys tore up the coast road, or at least Jeremy and Richard were. James, as usual, was struggling with speed and was being haunted by the American bike. Despite May's lack of speed though, it was actually Jeremy's bike that came to a stop, with the weed bag no longer doing the job. Despite his bike breaking down again, Clarkson couldn't have cared less as he ogled the fantastic view while they waited for James to catch up. It was at this moment, parked on the side of the mountain road, that Richard and James decided to give Jeremy a present in return, a painting of a traditional Vietnamese scene that was about 3ft square in size.

So, with Clarkson and his painting, Richard and his Galleon, and James with his ballet statue, they pushed on down the mountain towards Hué. By this time, Jeremy was really beginning to enjoy himself, event to the point of doing his own racing style commentary. James on the other hand, had made an observation, not a complaint, that when he backed down a gear, the breasts on his ballet statue would dig into his back. As the sun set in the distance, they stopped once more just to take in the beauty of Vietnam with Jeremy summing up the view. "It's a fabulous country, it really is."

That night, while Hammond was mending the masts on his sail ship, Jeremy and James took to his bike with bright pink spray paint. To avoid taking all the blame, they gave the spray paint to passersby and offered them the chance to do some of the painting. One of the many people even turned her sights on more than just Hammond's bike and continued to spray paint an unknown persons bicycle parked on the sidewalk.

In the morning, on the way to their next challenge, Hammond was furious with his new paint job, and began purposely side swiping anything he could to damage the Galleon on the back. Their next challenge was to take a Vietnamese driving test, which involved both theory and practical aspects. With only Jeremy knowing how to speak Vietnamese, the oral/theory side of the driving test was failed by both James and Richard. Outside the classroom, a number of different white lines were painted on the ground. These white lines made up a number of courses that would test the rider's ability to manoeuvre and maintain control of their bikes at slow speeds. One of the tests is to ride your bike around a figure of eight without touching the lines either on the inside or outside. Others include doing a full lock U-turn in a small box without touching any lines, and another is riding between two, very close, lines at a very slow speed. Hammond went first and with years of experience on motorbikes, passed with flying colours... or a pink bike at least. James was next and also passed drawing on his years of experience too. Clarkson however, due to his lack of experience, failed miserably, over and over again. He even tried using May's motorbike, and still failed, and when parking the motorbike without using the stand, the ballet statue strapped on the back was broken. After agreeing that collectively, they had passed the test, Jeremy apologised to James and bought him a bouquet of flowers to stick on the front of his motorcycle before heading out of Huế.

On the way out of Huế, they made a brief stop at some unrestored gates of one of the few Vietnam Citadel sites built in the early 1800's. Now littered with bullet holes, the gates show that nothing is untouched by war. Still 400 miles away from the finish line, Jeremy discovered that the traffic was getting worse, the weather was getting hotter and even James' bike was ready to give up. While stopped for lunch, Jeremy did his calculations and worked out that they simply could not reach the finish line in the time frame they were given. His solution was simple, and typical of Clarkson, cheat. So they boarded an overnight train headed for Hạ Long City. James, in his infinite wisdom, had purchased tickets for 3rd class and Jeremy wasn't overly impressed with having to spend 13 hours on hard wooden chairs. To pass the time, they agreed to repair each other's gifts. Hammond placed a new piece of canvas over the hole in Jeremy's painting, May attempted to untangle the ropes on Hammond's sail ship, and Jeremy used his Doctorate in Engineering to put May's statue back together. In the morning, Clarkson proudly presented the statue back to James, after having used half a tub of glue and a roll of sticky tape to hold it together. Hammond had painted a Land Rover in the middle of Clarkson's Vietnamese painting, and James had turned Hammond's Galleon into a Chinese row boat by using some chopsticks and other decorative pieces.

Upon arrival at what the boys thought was Hạ Long City, they quickly noticed that they had instead jumped on the wrong train and ended up miles away in Hà Nội. Once the arguing stopped, they got back on their bikes and continued East to Hạ Long City, stopping for breakfast, dodging traffic and even passing the wreckage of a shot down B-52 Bomber. After getting lost trying to find the main road out of Hà Nội, they found their way on to what seemed to be a main road and were filled with confidence again. Clarkson took the time to share his thoughts on motorbikes in general. "I've always said to my children that if they buy a bike I will burn it, and if they replace it with another one, I shall burn that too. Now however, if they buy a bike I will completely understand… and then I'll burn it".

50 miles from Hạ Long City, Hammond's Minsk broke down again. James volunteered to help out while Jeremy kept on going. Whilst trying to fix the Minsk, Hammond hit the kick start while in gear and the bike fell over with Hammond landing had first in between May's legs. James commented, "You simultaneously head butted me in the gentleman's region and snapped the bow off the Galleon". Shortly after the head butt to the crotch, inevitably, Clarkson fell off his motorbike while going rather quickly. Despite having a bit of gravel rash, 2 broken ribs and a sore foot, Jeremy seemed to be more worried about his suit. Completely oblivious to Jeremy's accident, James and Richard were still buying each other ridiculous presents. After getting back on his bike, Jeremy caught up to James and Richard, who had passed him unknowingly, and began to shout abuse at them for choosing bikes in the first place. Jeremy again took the time to comment on the trip, "What a journey, 700 miles on my bike, 250 miles on a train, and about 50 miles on my face".

They eventually arrived in Hạ Long City and instantly began celebrating the completion of their journey. The celebration was short lived though, as one last challenge was handed to them. The challenge explained to them that they had not yet reached the final checkpoint, and that in order to reach it, they would need to convert their motorbikes to be able to travel across water. Their destination was Ba Hàng Bar, a floating bar, unreachable by land, located in between the 1,969 islands that make up Hạ Long Bay.

With little enthusiasm this time, they set off to find a workshop to make their bikes float. A montage is shown of the boys planning, preparing and building their "Bike-ski's". In the morning, the boys met at the beach where they would launch and did a final check before heading out on to the bay. James had almost dismantled his bike completely and rigged bits and pieces of his bike to a traditional Vietnamese fishing boat, attaching a long propeller shaft to the engine to power the craft. Richard kept the majority of his Minsk in one piece, adding a propeller for propulsion, rigging the handlebars to steer a rudder at the rear, and putting a great big swan head on the front of a raft. Jeremy perhaps had the most strangest idea, stringing together 4 canoe's by means of a welded frame and strapping his bike to the top with the engine powering two paddle steamer type wheels at the back. After James started Jeremy's engine for him, due to his injuries, the three of them set off. Richard's creation seemed fine at first, Jeremy's Bike-ski oddly enough, worked as well, but James struggled to get his to steer much at all and eventually crashed in to Jeremy, then crashed into some netting, and eventually started to sink. James had his Bike-ski towed back to the beach and began fitting some of Hammond's spare pontoons to his craft while Hammond and Clarkson pushed on ahead. Jeremy's first stroke of bad luck on the water came when he stalled his Vespa and needed Richard to help him kick start the bike again, the whole process wasn't entirely smooth with them both nearly crashing into one of the islands.

In their search for the bar, Jeremy and Richard had gotten bored and decided to look in some of the caves. It wasn't until they reached a point where they could go no further that they realised neither of their bikes had reverse gear. While they were struggling to get out of the cave, James had struck trouble yet again, with one of his pontoons coming loose. Jeremy and Richard eventually got free of the cave but didn't get far when Jeremy's electrical system shorted on the bike and began running a current through anything metal, including the frame which bolted the bike to the canoe's, and the bike frame itself. James continued on with only one pontoon and even Richard had a spot of trouble when his rudder broke, sending his Bike-ski around in circles.

Jeremy continued on with his little Vespa and managed to arrive at Ba Hàng Bar first. Much later, despite steering troubles, Hammond somehow managed to get his Minsk within metres of the Bar, only Jeremy refused to help him get any closer. He eventually resorted to using his hands to paddle the water and help steer the bike towards the Bar, finally being able to grab the side of the floating pontoons. May, would be the last to arrive, struggling to get his bike away from one of the islands in time resulted in him getting stuck without a reverse gear. With Richard by his side to enjoy a drink, Jeremy shared some knowledge that he had learned of the people who live aboard the floating buildings. "The people who live here are born here, they live here, they fish here, and they die here. They never go on dry land".

James eventually made it off the side of the island and edged his way closer to the bar before losing the only pontoon he had left keeping his bike afloat, and to top it all off, the engine stalled on him too. While trying desperately to get his bike going again, he fell overboard and decided to just swim to the floating bar with the aid of the pontoon that fell off earlier. As he reached the side of the bar, Jeremy and Richard began laughing when James presented the item he salvaged from his Bike-ski before abandoning it, the ballet statue that was given to him as a present a few days ago.

Jeremy summed up the entire trip while clips of the past few days were shown. "I have to say though, that despite the success, I'm still not sold on biking. There are good moments, but it's mostly bad. And I'm sorry, but our machines were completely over-shadowed by this incredible, beautiful, brilliant country. It's hard to sum it up really, perhaps that's why people, when they get back from this place, always say the same thing – Vietnam, you don't know man, you weren't there!"

In typical Top Gear style, they added a particular something to the front of all the names in the credits. In this case, it was the name Francis Ford, a reference to Francis Ford Coppola, director of the famed Vietnam War film, Apocalypse Now.

Series 13

The thirteenth series of Top Gear started airing on 21 June 2009, with the usual presenting team of Jeremy Clarkson, Richard Hammond, James May and The Stig. The series contained 7 episodes. Despite forced budget cuts, series 13 contained new challenges, new power tests, more foreign travel and more races. Features include the Top Gear Race to the North, a race from London to Edinburgh between steam locomotive No. 60163 Tornado with Jeremy riding in the cab of the train, James May in a Jaguar XK120 and Richard Hammond on a Vincent Black Shadow motorbike, Richard and James racing a letter sent by the Royal Mail in a Porsche Panamera, and a review of the best cars for 17-year-olds. Glamour model and Page 3 girl Madison Welch also made an appearance in the sixth episode.

Episode	Reviews	Challenges	Star in a Reasonably Priced Car
1 21/06/2009	Lotus Evora • Ferrari FXX	Race to the North: (Jaguar XK120 vs. Vincent Black Shadow vs. Tornado locomotive)	Michael Schumacher (DNF)
2 28/06/2009	Lamborghini Murciélago LP 670-4 SV	Perfect £2,500 car for 17 year-olds • Drag Race: (Mercedes-Benz SLR McLaren 722 Edition vs. Lamborghini Murciélago LP 670-4 SV)• Drag Race II: (Bugatti Veyron vs. McLaren F1)	Stephen Fry (1:51 hot)

3 05/07/2009	Mercedes-Benz SL65 AMG Black Series	Search for a Cheap and cheerful car: (Proton Satria Neo • Chevrolet Aveo • Perodua Myvi • Fiat 500 • Toyota iQ • Alfa Romeo MiTo • Škoda Roomster) • Gymkhana rallying on the airfield (Subaru Impreza WRX STI)	Michael McIntyre (1:48.7)
4 12/07.2009	Ford Focus RS vs Renault Mégane R26.R	Race: (Porsche Panamera S vs. the Royal Mail service) • Playing British Bulldogs with live fire against the British Army in a Usain Bolt Mitsubishi Lancer Evolution VII	Usain Bolt (1:46.5)
5 19/07/2009	Jaguar XFR vs. BMW M5	Proof of three £1500 rear-wheel drive coupés better than front-wheel drive (Porsche 944 S2, Nissan 300ZX, Ford Capri 2.8i, Morris Marina) • Jeremy's inspired greenhouse trailer design to save the world	Sienna Miller (1:49.8)

6 26/08/2009	BMW Z4 sDrive35i • Nissan 370Z	Pre-1982 £3000 classic cars for a TSD rally in Mallorca (Austin-Healey Sprite, Lanchester LJ 200, Citroën Ami)	Brian Johnson (1:45.85)
7 02/09/2009	Vauxhall VXR8 Bathurst • HSV Maloo • Aston Martin V12 Vantage • Audi S4	Producing Volkswagen Scirocco adverts	Jay Leno (1:48.8)

Lamborghini Murcielago LP 670-4 SV

Richard goes to Abu Dhabi in the UAE to drive the new Lamborghini
Murcielago LP670-4 SV, the fastest Lamborghini ever made. The local
police have kindly closed a four mile straight stretch of highway for the car
to be tested on. Richard goes for a speed run and nudges 200mph on the first
run. From every angle, the car exudes menace, with 670hp and 4-wheel
drive it is extremely fast, and to help things along it is 100kg lighter than the
standard car. 0-60mph is dispatched in 3.2 seconds, and the LP670-4
eventually tops out at 212mph. Richard is amazed by the steering and the
way the car is light and nimble on its feet. While it may set you back
£270,000, Richard believes that it's cheap, considering it should be able to
match the best hyper cars available. Richard lines it up against a McLaren
Mercedes SLR 722 for a drag race. While the Murcielago lost the race, it
was extremely close at barely 2 car lengths in it after a mile. Very
impressive considering the SLR 722 is £100,000 more expensive. Back in
the studio, Richard and Jeremy discuss the magnificence of the car before
the Stig takes it for a lap. The Murcielago LP670-4 SV laps the track in
1:19.00.

Classic Car Challenge

The team was told to go to a classic car auction with £3,000 to buy a pre-1982 car. Richard, who claimed he was 'going ugly early' brought the first lot, a 1953 Lanchester Fourteen, Jeremy bought the first convertible for sale, a 1969 Austin-Healey Sprite Mark IV, which Richard kept calling a MG Midget, for £3,600, so he reluctantly had to spend £600 of his own money on it, and James, after being cautious and being outbid on a Bristol 401, reluctantly had to buy the last item, a 1976 Citroën Ami, which was equipped with a starter handle inserted into the front of the car. After buying their cars, they were told to go to Majorca for the Rally Clásico Isla Mallorca (Majorca Classic Car Rally), a classic car regularity rally. Before they went though, Hammond, who repeatedly claimed that his grandfather had made his car, had to get his car an MOT. This proved difficult, as shown later in the show his long list of errors with the car.

After getting his car an MOT, Richard had run out of money to spend on preparing for the rally. Jeremy had removed the roof and painted green racing stripes down his car and inserted racing seats and a roll-bar, and James had fitted a spare tyre and shovel. They were told to race around a set route passing checkpoints at a set average speed of 50 km/h (31 mph) on public roads with traffic. Points were given for going too fast/too slow, and the one with the fewest points won. The producers had also chosen their assistant drivers. Jeremy was given Joan Verger, the head of the Balearic Motorsport Federation and former SEAT works driver, who knew the roads well but didn't speak English. Richard was given an English mechanic, Brian Wheeler, who is a little person, and ironically James was given glamour model and Page 3 girl Madison Welch. Jeremy bet £25 that he'd win, which the other two agreed with. At the rally there were many better cars, such as a Lancia Stratos, Lancia Delta, Ford Mustang and many Porsche 911s. The co-drivers proved troublesome, as Jeremy struggled to communicate, Richard constantly and accidentally offended Brian with 'short' quips, and Madison was being very uncooperative and didn't know much about car rallying. Jeremy won the challenge, with around 3,000 penalty points, by going too fast initially before reducing his speed due to a clutch fault. James came second with around 44,000 points, and Richard came last with 47,000 as he had frequent breakdowns, the lowest score ever in rallying history.

The next and final challenge was to run 3 Laps round a race track at the same lap time in all 3 laps. Everyone understood, except Jeremy who asked seriously, "If you break down, do you then have to repeatedly break down on the other 2 laps?" Jeremy did 2 very smooth laps at similar speeds, but on his final lap he went mad and raced a Ford Mustang who overtook him, as he said being overtaken is a sign of weakness, and James did 3 laps at the same time "to the nearest second." At the end of the show, it was revealed that James had won in his Citroën Ami, therefore getting £50. After the races, James and Madison are seen having lunch on a picnic blanket. In voice over, Clarkson said, "All of us, in our own way… had fallen a little bit in love."

At the end of the show, Jeremy said that all three of them loved their cars so much that they actually bought them for themselves off the BBC. Jeremy then revealed to Richard that he knew all along that the Lanchester in question was actually built at a factory in Wales, meaning that while someone's grandfather probably worked on it, it certainly wasn't Richard's.

Aston Martin V12 Vantage

Jeremy drives the Aston Martin V12 Vantage, a modified version of the V8 Vantage with a V12 engine pulled from the Aston Martin DBS V12. The feature shows a montage of rolling and interior shots of the Vantage, with Clarkson remarking very little on the car itself (he says it is an Aston Martin Vantage with a V12 engine, what do you think it's going to be like? Stating that it should cover everything he desires.), and more about how various factors such as the Environment, the Economy, the war on speed and problems in the Middle East mean that in the future such cars will be consigned to the history books. Clarkson ends the series by simply saying 'Goodnight', as the credits roll over continuing shots of the Vantage driving through mountainous British countryside.

Series 14

The fourteenth series of Top Gear started airing on BBC Two and BBC HD on the 15th of November 2009. The series contained 7 episodes. Episode 1 featured the team being sent to find the Transfăgărăşan road in Romania with Jeremy in an Aston Martin DBS Volante, Richard in a Ferrari California and James in a Lamborghini Gallardo LP560-4 Spyder. Episode 2 featured Jeremy, Richard and James attempting to build an electric car better than a G-Wiz. Episode 3 featured a road trip between James May in a caravan airship and Richard Hammond in a Lamborghini Balboni. Episode 4 featured a road test of Renault Twingo RS 133, before being driven off the docks in Belfast. Episode 5 featured Jeremy, James and Richard taking over an art gallery in Middlesbrough and filling it with motoring-related works, in attempt to prove "cars can be art too". In the style of their trips to Vietnam, Botswana, the North Pole and the United States, Episode 6 was a 75-minute special from Bolivia. Episode 7 featured Jeremy's worldwide review of the BMW X6, including visits to Hong Kong (to find a metaphor that describes the car), Spain (to test if the suspension is better on Spanish roads), Barbados (to work out if the car is better than a tropical holiday) and Australia (to test if the glove box still works).

Episode	Reviews	Challenges	Star in a Reasonably Priced Car
1 15/11/2009	BMW 760Li • Mercedes-Benz S63 AMG • Lamborghini Gallardo LP560-4 Spyder • Ferrari California • Aston Martin DBS Volante	Romanian GT road trip to find the Transfăgărăşan highway (Dacia Sandero)	1:47.5 – Eric Bana (wet)
2 22/11/2009	Chevrolet Corvette C6 ZR1 vs. Audi R8 V10	Codename Geoff / Hammerhead Eagle-i Thrust vs. G-Wiz • Build an electric car	1:46.3 – Michael Sheen

		better than a G-Wiz	
3 29/11/2009	Why Lancia has made greatest number of great cars: (Lancia Stratos HF • Lancia Delta HF Integrale Evo II)	Lamborghini Gallardo LP550-2 Valentino Balboni • Fly an Airship caravan	20.1:48.1 – Chris Evans (wet)
4 06/12/2009	BMW X5 M • Audi Q7 V12 TDI • Range Rover (2010MY)	Airport vehicle motorsport • Renault Twingo 133 barrel roll in a tunnel	1:52.5 – Guy Ritchie (wet)
5 20/12/2009	Noble M600	Make an automotive art gallery to prove cars are more popular than traditional art	Jenson Button (1:44.9)
6 27/12/2009	None	Bolivia Special	None
7 03/01/2010	Lexus LFA	'Low-budget' worldwide review of the BMW X6 • Vauxhall Insignia VXR • May and	1.51.8 – Seasick Steve (moist)

		Margaret Calvert reflect on the evolution of UK road signs • Top Gear Awards 2009	

Romanian GT Road Trip

Jeremy (in an Aston Martin DBS Volante), Richard (in a Ferrari California), and James (in a Lamborghini Gallardo LP560-4 Spyder) are sent to find the world's greatest driving road, which apparently is in Romania and called the "Transfăgărăşan". Along the way they have races along Romania's Motorways, have a sat-nav race to the People's Palace, race under the People's Palace, smash up a Dacia Sandero, travel through the rural Romanian countryside, crash James' Lamborghini and sleep beside an enormous dam (the Vidraru Dam). Clarkson insists that the Aston is the best grand tourer, to which James and Richard disagree.

Lancia Stratos

Jeremy and Richard review different cars from the Lancia car company which they declared had the greatest number of great cars. Despite the ruined reputation Lancia had because of the rusty Beta saloons, Jeremy and Richard loved the cars Lancia made. The Stig then did a power lap with a Hawk HF3000 (a continuation car of the Lancia Stratos), which broke down on its first attempt. When it was finally fixed, the car's lack of traction and the very wet conditions combined to make the Stig spin out twice during the lap (in Chicago and the Second to the Last Corner), giving the Hawk Stratos the slowest power lap in the show's history at 1:48.2.

Top Gear Bolivia Special

Jeremy, Richard and James travel 1,000 miles through South America from the rainforests of Bolivia to the Pacific coast of Chile. The presenters used second hand off-road vehicles, bought locally in Bolivia for less than £3,500 each.

Richard bought a tan Toyota Land Cruiser which had been converted into a soft top convertible by a previous owner. However, part of the soft top was set alight when Clarkson used an angle grinder to cut air vents in the bonnet of his Range Rover to cool the engine. Despite the Toyota's reputation for durability, it turned out to be the most unreliable car, suffering multiple drivetrain and suspension breakdowns right from the start. The Toyota, already in terrible condition, underwent modifications towards the end of the trip and was made a lot heavier than before- these additions put considerable stress on the drivetrain and made the car even less reliable. It was eventually converted to front-wheel drive after the rear prop shaft broke off, destroying the rear differential. It was damaged beyond repair on the sand-dune descent. His car was nicknamed the "Donkey."

Jeremy bought a red Range Rover which he believed had a 3.9 litre fuel injected engine. However, when he showed his co-presenters under the bonnet, May noted it had carburetors, making it the 3.5 litre model. It became notorious for overheating and stopped working on some occasions, but it was very capable of dealing with the rough terrain. However, during the trip, none of the Range Rover's features were shown to be working, "apart from the de-mist!" Like Hammond's Toyota, it underwent modifications to handle the high-altitude part of the trip. Unlike the Toyota, however, it survived the trip, and was declared the winner, much to the amusement of the presenters, who had previously deemed it the most unreliable car, hence Clarkson's conclusion that "the most unreliable car in the world is the most reliable car in the world."

James bought a Suzuki SJ413 which "...was blue in the picture," but red when delivered. The Suzuki Samurai had a 1.3 litre engine, was the smallest of the three vehicles. Despite this, it did not undergo modifications, and broke down the least (the main reason for it breaking down was when water entered the fuel tank while fording the jungle river). One disadvantage of this vehicle was its broken 4-wheel drive system, which made it a "3-wheel drive system;" May had not engaged one of the free-wheeling hubs to the lock position. Another major problem was that the alternator was broken, requiring his car battery to be swapped with Hammond's. It was still a very capable off-roader, especially when its small engine and size are considered, though Clarkson's Range Rover was still declared to be the ultimate winner.

The three presenters started at a riverside in the Amazon jungle where a towed river raft left their cars (the presenters were supposed to have been "helicoptered" in to the location, but Clarkson said that the helicopter had crashed before filming, necessitating a boat trip up the river). The trio were originally left on the bank with nothing. Hammond remarked on the other two's inappropriate clothing and they all revealed their phobias. Hammond is terrified of insects, James May is scared of heights and Clarkson, manual labour, something May says is just 'bone idleness.' After doing nothing for a long time, a raft finally arrives with their cars. The driver of the raft only parks it vaguely near the bank, so, at that point, they cannot disembark.

While trying to move the raft, Clarkson started to sink into the mudflats in the river and so Hammond had to pull him out with Clarkson's Range Rover. They had trouble getting the cars off the raft, as Hammond's car wouldn't start and the raft was too small for Clarkson to give him a push-start. It was not until the next morning that May realised that some of the planks were long enough to make a ramp off the raft. James tried to get off the raft first, but got stuck up a small hill just after the ramp. As May was blocking the path, they had to get a third plank to get Clarkson off the raft. He managed, and also pulled May's Suzuki up the hill, and into a log. Clarkson also had to tow Hammond off the raft, and then give him a pull-start.

For the first section of the journey, they were forced to make a route by slashing undergrowth and went along logging trails, encountering snakes and insects. During this segment, several fan blades were broken off Clarkson's engine fan, later leading to him cutting holes in the bonnet for additional ventilation. This unfortunately resulted in the roof of Hammond's Toyota catching fire. Clarkson tried to drive across a small gully, but failed. May tried to winch him out, but ended up pulling his own vehicle into the gully, so Hammond had to winch both of their vehicles back to the starting point. A chainsaw and rope were used to make a bridge out of the trunks of four young trees to complete the crossing. For the next section, the cars underwent minor modifications to cross a river, including non-standard use of certain products including tampons to waterproof a fuel tank cap, and Vaseline and Condoms to waterproof parts of the engine. Hammond got through the river without problems. Clarkson, however, stalled, so May had to drive around him, and he got stuck. As Hammond was winching May out, Clarkson got his car started without any problems, which seriously annoyed May. In the director's cut, they encounter a tree fall in the middle of the road, which Hammond and May work at with machetes for "two hours" Clarkson promptly comes in with the chainsaw which gets stuck. After sawing through the log, he starts to saw at James' car. The chainsaw breaks down, and Hammond and May, thinks the chainsaw breaking down is possibly a message from god, that the ever technical handicapped Jezza, should not play around with it.

They then climbed the Andes to La Paz along the Yungas Road, also known as the 'Death Road' because of its narrowness and sheer drops. Due to May's fear of heights, he threatened to cut anyone's head off if they bumped into him, later waving a machete near Clarkson's face when he bumped him by accident. (As per the running gag in Top Gear Hammond had been repeatedly bumping May before the warning). Later, Hammond drove into a ditch to avoid a passing bus, and found out that May's car's winch was broken. Elsewhere, Clarkson was placed in extreme danger when he met a car coming the other way on a particularly narrow section of the road, and the edge of the road ledge started to crumble under his wheels. Near the end of the section, Clarkson held a brief memorial service for Hammond and May, jokingly suggesting that they must be dead. He put two makeshift crosses up, labelling one 'Ted Nugent' and the other 'Ray Mears'.

They modified their cars in La Paz: Clarkson and Hammond fitted much bigger wheels and tyres on their cars, which had a negative effect on their performance, because it geared up the cars too much for their gearboxes. Hammond also got rid of the roof, and replaced it with a lighter rollbar. May simply 'mended' his car. Afterwards, they crossed the Altiplano while using a portable GPS with an altitude readout. They tried to take a straight route into Chile over the Guatllatiri active volcano. This attempt was defeated by weakness and a drunken-type feeling after about 16,000 feet caused by severe hypoxia, the result of being at such a high altitude. They had each taken a Viagra tablet to try to prevent high altitude pulmonary edema (HAPE) from altitude hypoxia. Altitude hypoxia also much reduced the cars' effective power, which meant May's car could produce no more than 20 bhp. On the way, they passed at least two active volcanic steam vents. At 17,200 feet altitude (3.26 miles, 5,243 metres, where the air pressure was about half an atmosphere), they stopped and appraised their current medical state. All three were displaying clear signs of altitude sickness and as the road was continuing to climb, the trio decided to turn back and take a lower route. During the climb, they used a pulse oximeter to read their blood oxygen saturation, which sometimes was down to 84%, a value which in normal life would recommend admission to hospital.

A few miles from the end of their journey, the route took them down a very steep sand dune to reach the Pacific coast, on Caleta Los Verdes, some 20 kilometres south of Iquique, Chile. They initially decided to practice on a less steep dune. Just prior to starting their practice run, Hammond got out to talk to Clarkson, 'forgetting' that his handbrake was broken and that he had left the Toyota in neutral (A hand can be seen through the Toyota window letting go of the car at the rear, causing it to begin moving forward). The Toyota began rolling down the dune driverless and rolled over, losing a wheel in the process. The broken wheel hub meant the end for the Toyota, but Clarkson and May completed the dangerous descent to the coastline.

Although Hammond was forced to admit the defeat of the Toyota Land Cruiser that he lovingly referred to as "The Donkey", he still argued that he had chosen wisely. Clarkson observed that May's Suzuki may have completed the journey, but it had been a very rough ride; May agreed, saying, "The ride is rotten". Due to the Toyota's failure and the Suzuki's hard ride, Clarkson declared that although the Range Rover was the most unreliable car in the world, it had proven itself to be the most reliable car in the world.

Although it was not mentioned on the show, some of the images show them passing along Lago Chyngara (approx 4600 m in elevation) and the Parincota Volcano near this lake in the Lauca National Park. These came into view just before the three began their drive up the Guallatiri volcano. This episode is regarded by the presenters as the best in show history.

Series 15

The fifteenth series of Top Gear started airing on BBC Two and BBC HD on the 27th of June 2010, and concluded on 1 August 2010,. Prior to the series, the channel advertised the show's return by featuring a home video originally published to YouTube. In the clip, the parents of a young boy see the Top Gear crew filming the motorhome challenge. The over-excited responses of the parents were adapted to produce the trailer. Several segments which were recorded for the series were missed out, including Jeremy travelling from the most westerly point at sunset to the most easterly point at sunrise in the new Jaguar XJ, and the return of Jonathan Ross to the reasonably priced car.

Episode	Reviews	Challenges	Star in a Reasonably Priced Car
1 27/06/2010	Bentley Continental Supersports	Toyota Hilux Invincible up an Icelandic volcano • Farewell to the former reasonably priced car, the Chevrolet Lacetti • Why Reliant went out of business: 1994 Reliant Robin	1:49.9 – Nick Robinson 1:48.1 – Al Murray 1:45.9 – Peter Jones 1:49.9 – Peta Todd (damp) 1:53.3 – Johnny Vaughan (wet)

			1:50.8 – Bill Bailey (wet)
			1:53.69 – Louie Spence (wet)
			36.1:50.9 – Amy Williams (wet)
2 04/07/2010	Porsche 911 Sport Classic • Porsche Boxster Spyder	Find a £5,000 everyday second-hand sports saloon for track days (Mercedes-Benz 190, BMW M3, Ford Sierra Sapphire RS Cosworth)	1:47.0 – Alastair Campbell
3 11/07/2010	Chevrolet Camaro SS vs. Mercedes-Benz E63 AMG	Find the greatest four-door supercar by driving wedding guests: (Aston Martin Rapide vs. Porsche Panamera Turbo vs. Maserati Quattroporte GTS)	1:45.5 – Rupert Grint 1:44.3 - Rubens Barrichello
4 18/07/2010	Audi R8 V10 Spyder vs. Porsche 911 Turbo Cabriolet	Building motorhomes on the back of a Land Rover 110, a Citroën CX and a Lotus Excel	1:46.1 – Andy García

5 25/07/2010	None	Volkswagen Touareg vs Swedish snowmobilers • Reach 258mph (415 km/h) in the Bugatti Veyron Super Sport • Commemorating racing driver Ayrton Senna, Tom Cruise • Cameron Diaz Lewis Hamilton drives his 1988 F1 racing car.	1:44.2 – Tom Cruise 1:45.2 – Cameron Diaz
6 01/08/2010	Ferrari 458 Italia	Old British roadsters for £5000: (Jensen-Healey, TVR S2, Lotus Elan)	1:49.0 – Jeff Goldblum

Reliant Robin

Jeremy moves on to the Reliant Robin, a car which was extremely popular even though it was made from plastic and cost more than a Mini when new. The reliant had a single wheel at the front, rather than at the rear like most other 3 wheelers. Jeremy has always been worried about this and is even more worried that his challenge today is to drive it from Sheffield to Rotherham, a distance of 14 miles. Jeremy sets off and straight away rolls the Robin onto its side coming out of the parking garage driveway. Phillip Oakey from the Human League helps Jeremy by pushing the car back onto its wheels. It isn't long before Jeremy almost rolls again, rolling the Robin onto its side on 45 degrees. But this time he discovers a useful feature of the car, opening the door can help lever the car back onto all 3 wheels, and he was on his way. Jeremy's Robin is a 1975 model and has an 850cc engine, which increased the top speed (from less than 60mph) to an incredibly scary 85mph. Jeremy rolls the car at speed across an intersection and is rescued by Peter Stringfellow, the owner of various lap dancing clubs. Jeremy rolls (literally) into a Reliant Robin car club meeting to chat with some enthusiasts about how to drive a Robin best, and why they were so popular. Afterwards, Jeremy gate crashes a news broadcast, gets stuck in a mechanic's inspection pit and interrupts a cricket match before ending the episode by crashing the Robin into a canal.

Bugatti Veyron Supersport

James moves on to the next segment by looking back at Top Gear's history with the Bugatti Veyron; "If you look back at all the amazing things we've done with the Bugatti Veyron, you could be forgiven for thinking that it's the fastest car on the planet. The fact is though, is isn't. Because this car will do 253mph, but there's now a car in America called the Shelby Ultimate Aero which will so 256mph, so that officially is the world's fastest production car." Bugatti were not pleased, so behind closed doors they created the Veyron Super Sport to become the undisputed fastest production car in the world. The Super Sport has the same 0-60mph time of 2.5 seconds is the same as the regular Veyron, but after that everything is utterly different. 0-100mph takes just 4.5 seconds and will go on to an alleged speed of 258mph. To achieve this extra 5mph, the Super Sport needs an extra 200bhp – bringing the total to 1,200bhp. The Super Sport also has a more slippery carbon fiber body and a price tag of £1,600,000. To attempt to reach the top speed, James goes once again to VW's test track, Ehra-Lessien, in Germany. The test track features a 5.5mile straight, one of very few places in the world where you can max a Bugatti Veyron. The engineers do their final check on the car and James ventures out onto the track. James drops down the gears gradually as he proceeds around the banked turn before entering the main straight at 125mph in third gear. The car is fitted with an accurate speedometer which measures in kph, so it reads 200kph at this time. He plants his foot and within seconds reaches 270kph, and 340kph a few seconds after. Within moments James reaches 400kph (248 mph) – and soon passes the top speed of the original Veyron, 407mph. To reach the Super Sport's top speed of 258mph, he would need to hit 415kph. James reached this speed and then went further to finish at 417mph (259mph). Back in the studio, James reveals that one of Bugatti's test drivers went out after him to have a try. To get the official speed record, the Super Sport had to be run in both directions and then the average between the two speeds is used. Bugatti's test driver set a record of an incredible 431kph, or 267mph. The Super Sport is then handed over to The Stig, to try break another record. The Stig smokes all four tyres off the line in a very aggressive dry lap, returning a time of 1:16.80 – the new fastest car ever around the Top Gear Test Track.

Ferrari 458 Italia

Jeremy goes out on the track with a new Ferrari – the 458 Italia. The 458 differs from the old F430 in a number of areas. The steering wheel features a confusing amount of controls – such as buttons for the indicators, wipers, headlights, suspension settings, headlight dim dip, traction control and the starter motor. Presumably this was due to the 458 having gearshift paddles and the designers wished to do away with the conventional indicator and wiper stalks, but this in itself creates some problems. Jeremy explains, "The thing about a steering wheel is, it moves. So none of the buttons are ever where you left them." If you wanted to indicate left midway through a corner for example, the left indicator button may actually be upside down on the right side of the wheel. The problems continue as two LCD displays sit either side of the central rev counter on the dashboard, the left displays car information such as fuel and tyre temperatures, with the one on the right either displaying the speedo or the satnav... but not both at once. Despite this, Jeremy suggests that the 458 Italia is the first properly pretty Ferrari we've seen since the 308 came along in 1975. Ferrari maintains they arrived at the design based on science, rather than purely for asthetics. The 458 Italia produces 562bhp, which is 79 more than the old F430. To demonstrate this difference in power, Jeremy has brought along James' very own F430 and puts it against the 458 Italia in a drag race. The 458 Italia has a 4.5L V8 which can do 0-60mph in 3.8 seconds and rev to 9000rpm – in the race it absolutely humiliates the F430.

Jeremy then ponders what the 458 is like as a driver's car, and goes on "You probably think it will be brilliant, you probably imagine all Ferrari's are magnificent when you put the hammer down, but again, the truth is.. they aren't. The 348 for example felt like it had tyres made from wood. The 275 had milk bottle tops for brakes. The engine in an F50 felt like it was bolted directly to your spine, and the 400 was simply awful in every way." Luckily however, the 458 Italia turns out to be brilliant, while power sliding it through the turns, Jeremy describes it as "being beyond anything" and that although it costs £170,000 which is a lot, he doesn't care because the 458 is one of the all time greats. He sums up the test by saying "It really is absolutely, unbelievably, mesmerizingly brilliant." Back in the studio, we see The Stig take it for a lap around a dry track. It returns a time of 1:19.10.

Series 16

The sixteenth series of Top Gear began airing on the 21st of December 2010.

Episode	Reviews	Challenges	Star in a Reasonably Priced Car
USA Road Trip 21/12/2010	None	USA Road Trip	1:47.8 – Danny Boyle (wet)
Middle East 26/12/2010	None	Middle East Special	None
1 23/01/2011	Ariel Atom V8 • Škoda Yeti	History of the Porsche 911: Porsche 911 Turbo S Cabriolet	1:42.8 – John Bishop
2 30/01/2011	Ferrari 599 GTO	Challenge vs Top Gear Australia in a motoring version of The Ashes.	1:45.9 – Boris Becker (wet)
3 06/02/2011	"Albania Road Trip": (Rolls-Royce Ghost • Yugo	Hatchbacks: (Ford Focus RS500 • Cosworth	1:49.0 – Jonathan Ross (wet)

	(substituting for a Bentley Mulsanne) • Mercedes-Benz S65 AMG)	Impreza STI CS400 • Volvo C30 PCP)	
4 13/02/2011	None	Second-hand, four seater convertibles • Pagani Zonda R • Pagani Zonda Tricolore	1:44.9 – Simon Pegg 1:44.5 – Nick Frost
5 20/02/2011	Audi RS5 • BMW M3 Competition Pack	Convert a combine harvester into a snow plough	1:50.3 – Amber Heard (automatic)
6 27/02/2011	Porsche 959 • Ferrari F40	Sunset to sunrise race in a Jaguar XJ 5.0 V8 Supersport across England • NASA's latest Space Exploration Vehicle	1.56.7 – John Prescott (wet + automatic)

Top Gear USA " Road Trip" Special

The team start off series 16 on the Transfagarasan Highway in Romania. A road which Top Gear discovered a few years ago and promptly called "The best road in the world". However letters from a bunch of Americans seem to suggest that the Blue Ridge Parkway in Virginia, USA, is actually better. So Jeremy, Richard and James each chose a car and went over to check it out. James selected a Ferrari 458 Italia; Jeremy, a Mercedes SLS, with Richard ending up in a Porsche 911 GT3 RS. After an argument over who had brought the best car, they set off along the Blue Ridge Parkway to let the road decide... however, immediately there was a problem. The speed limit along this truly stunning piece of road is just 35mph. After some time it reduced to 25mph so the boys pulled over for an emergency meeting. Continuing along the Parkway would be pointless, as it is 469 miles long. Turning off to the left would mean they'd end up in the woods of North Carolina, whilst turning right would have them heading straight into the heart of NASCAR country. They chose the latter.

Once they got out and turned onto the highway, they all went a bit mad and unleashed a bit of pent up speed. Jeremy explains why he loves the SLS so much – "This may look and sound like a muscle car, but underneath its very technical, it's very European. The gearbox is at the back for better weight distribution – and it's the same double clutch 7-speed box that Ferrari used in the California". Richard goes into bat for his Porsche – "This isn't a Super car, it's a sports car. It's been stripped out and lightened. It sacrifices rear seats, yes, but it just feels alive. Pure, direct, immediate". James however was struggling a bit with the steering wheel in the 458 – which has a baffling amount of controls on it. The boys continue along until they reach the birthplace of NASCAR, North Wilkesboro Speedway. America's first oval track. Today it lays in a state of disrepair with rough tarmac and overgrown grandstands. After swearing to the Mayor that they wouldn't go fast, the boys take to the track with their cars. But rather quickly it turns into a bit of a race. Jeremy goes overboard and manages to get the SLS drifting – eventually shredding a rear tyre after only a few laps. The Mayor gets on the phone to try and find a shop which could fit a new tyre to the SLS – as it doesn't carry a spare. Richard and James depart to leave Jeremy to fend for himself. Two tyre shops later and still without success, Jeremy is forced to drive the final 115 miles in the dark to the hotel on a ruined tyre.

Later it turns out Jeremy did make it to the hotel successfully – which turned out to be a motor racing resort right beside Virginia International Raceway. Shortly after a morning cup of tea, Jeremy was able to get new tyres for the SLS and the boys hit the track. Jeremy couldn't keep up with Richard and James and decides that it would be more fun going slowly and drifting just like the day before. Richard's GT3 RS may have 110bhp less than the 458 Italia, but even so he set about trying to catch up to James, who was driving like a "scolded proverbial". Richard slowly began to close in on James – losing ground on the straights but catching back up again through the corners. The race was starting to get very serious, with the boys pushing harder and harder – until Richard eventually caught right up to the back of James' 458. Richard pushed the GT3 a little too hard around a high speed corner which caused the back of the car to step out, sending him spearing across the grass towards a tyre wall. Luckily he pulled up just in time to avoid it.

For the next challenge, the boys do a drive by shooting – firing at a target through the passenger window as an instructor drives along. Due to a recent book release by The Stig (Ben Collins), cardboard cutouts of him are selected to be the target in question. James and Richard both do a drive by each using a pistol – followed by Jeremy in the SLS – who had the unfair advantage of being able to lift up the entire door and sit on the sill for a clearer shot with an assault rifle. After the scores were tallied up, Jeremy won the event with 245, followed by Richard in second with 145, and James third at 82. The next morning, the boys hit the road and head for New York City – which would take a surprisingly long time due to the slow speed limits on the road. To cure the boredom, the boys decide to have races from 45 to 55 mph. This keeps them entertained until lunch time, when they try to find a restaurant using the SatNav in Jeremy's SLS. This fails to find anything except fast food restaurants. After lunch at McDonalds, the boys make a slight detour through Washington DC, before finding a drag racing circuit so Jeremy & James could settle the argument as to who had the fastest car. On a soaking wet track, neither driver was able to get the power down without spinning the wheels. On the final run James applies the throttle a bit more gently and manages to actually complete a run without spinning – making him the winner.

As they approach New York City, where they gather under the Manhattan Bridge to receive their next challenge. Jeremy reads it out – "You have been booked to appear at 11am on an American Chat show. The studio is on West 59th St, near its junction with 11th Avenue. There's only time for one of you to appear so the first to arrive gets the gig." Jeremy and James decide to use their Satnav and spend a few minutes trying to find the address. Richard's GT3 RS doesn't have one, so he sets off first to get a head start and consults his printed map on the way. Jeremy and James both get slightly lost and also frustrated by New York's many one-way streets. James ends up going too far, but manages to backtrack to the studio and arrives first, followed by Jeremy soon after and Richard a distant last place. Not that they envied James – the TV show in question ended up being an aerobics programme on the Manhattan Neighborhood Network.

Top Gear Middle East Special

Jeremy, Richard and James are given a challenge to re-enact the journey of the three wise men, by traveling from northern Iraq to a stable in Bethlehem in £3500 convertibles. As Israel will not allow cars registered in its surrounding neighbours to enter its borders, they must buy cars from Georgia before flying to their destination in the back of a Russian cargo plane. Whilst the plane is in flight, Richard introduces us to the car he has purchased, a Fiat Barchetta Riviera Special. Jeremy suggests that Richard has been stupid – and that no Fiat would be reliable enough to complete the journey. Compared to Richard's brave choice, Jeremy played it safe and brought along a Mazda MX5. He explains "Every time we do one of these trips, every time I get the interesting car, it's in a cloud of steam. This time, wherever we're going, this will make it." Lastly, James shows us his BMW Z3 – on which he went £466 over budget.

Still oblivious to where they are going, the boys strap into their cars to get ready for landing. While on final approach the captain opens the rear cargo doors, leaving Richard screaming as he stared out at the expansive desert in front of him. To make matters worse, the pilot is forced to abort the first landing and circle around for another attempt – all the time with the doors still open. Eventually the plane lands and the boys find out that they're actually in Iraq. Donning flak jackets and helmets they quickly drive out of the plane and take refuge in a nearby airport hangar. There, they break out a map and decide that it is too dangerous to drive directly to Bethlehem, as it would involve traveling through the heart of Iraq and past the Al-Qaeda stronghold of Mosul. Instead, Jeremy proposes a much longer route that involves traveling east and crossing into Iran and then doubling back into Turkey and down through Syria to avoid Iraq almost entirely.

After setting off the boys get slightly lost and end up going through a series of dusty alley ways which make them feel a bit vulnerable. After getting back to the busy main road, James' BMW decides to break down. He positions the car over a nearby open sewer to use as a makeshift inspection pit – and tells the others to go away. Jeremy however is reluctant, "I was just thinking, I know we're not supposed to just wander off, but it's Iraq – right there. You stand here and there's a kitchen supplier here, and there's a school boy there with his tie on, and everything's normal. But it just takes one person and then it's not a normal place at all." James eventually gets the Z3 going again but not for long – he therefore takes it to a workshop where they discover the problem is actually a blown head gasket. The next day, with the BMW fixed, the trio finally leave Erbil and continue through the countryside and the frequent military checkpoints. Soon after it begins to rain and the road becomes incredibly slippery. Jeremy spins his MX5 going down a perfectly straight bit of road. But it wasn't just the roads which were dangerous – the next section went through a mountain range close to the Iranian border. James describes it as "Bandit country" and the boys proceed with caution.

Whilst stopping for a rest, Jeremy shared a brainwave he had – "I know how to make my car bulletproof. I am going to take the door linings off and fill the doors with sand. Put the door linings back on so you're driving around with two sand bags on either side of you." James is very doubtful of this, so Jeremy finds a quiet spot to try it out. He shovels some sand into the door and also stuffs in a few sand filled plastic bags. Top Gear's armed escort steps in and fires a round through the door to see how well Jeremy's idea has worked. Upon inspection, the bullet hit the door and then split into multiple pieces, which kept going through the car before exiting through the door on the opposite side making several large holes – a dismal failure. They hit the road again and by nightfall the boys reach the Iranian border, where they discover that due to "political reasons" that the BBC is not permitted to cross into Iran. With no other options, they decide to head back across Iraq and find a route to the Turkish border and hopefully bypass Mosul. The boys drive into the night but eventually stop and stay the night at an Iraqi amusement park. The next morning whilst they sampled some of the rides, they had an epiphany. Jeremy, Richard and James had been in Iraq for 2 days and they hadn't been shot even once, or blown up, or be-headed on the internet. So they decided to remove their helmets and flak jackets and hit the mountain roads again – this time while actually enjoying it.

By midday they reach the Turkish border. After a few hours clearing customs, they discover that they now had an even bigger problem. The producers inform them that the Kurdish insurgency is attempting to reclaim the southern provinces of Turkey and that the region has been declared a war zone. They are given four hours to travel the two hundred miles to a hotel in the safe zone before nightfall. They hit the road, fast. But this didn't bode well for Jeremy's MX5. After pushing his car too hard, one of the spark plugs pops out and turns the engine into a 3-cylinder. After gluing it back in them continue on their way and make it to the hotel well after nightfall. That night, to punish Richard for being smug about his car's reliability – Jeremy and James install a secret stereo in the Fiat and load up a Genesis CD – a band Hammond is known to hate. The original stereo is unplugged, giving him no idea how to turn the sound down. Not a good morning to be playing jokes on Richard however – he reveals he has had "the trots" since 3am in the morning. They finally turn south and cross the Syrian border. Their progress was halted briefly by the security system in James' Z3 – which had completely immobilised the engine. Once inside, they discover that Top Gear is enormously popular in Syria – which is not great because Israel will not allow them into the country if the authorities know they have been in Syria. Jeremy proposes that the "sneak through" Syria by modifying their cars for desert travel and avoid the main roads. After a night of modifications, Richard unveils his Fiat Bedouin tent. Jeremy paints his car in bright colours to resemble Joseph and the Amazing Technicolor Dreamcoat -he also installs an "Axle of Evil" to make his Mazda a six-wheeled vehicle. Meanwhile, James takes inspiration from the Afrika Korps and models his BMW on a desert army unit.

While travelling through the desert, Richard's Fiat takes a battering and his radiator almost falls through the bottom of the car after its support is damaged. Jeremy gets bitten by an unidentified insect that causes his arm to swell up. Of more concern though is that James gets knocked over while hanging onto a snatch strap, as Richard attempts to pull Jeremy's MX5 out of a sand trap. His head gets cut on a rock and he seems to suffer from some short term memory loss. James is taken to a nearby hospital leaving Jeremy and Richard to carry on by themselves. The terrain gets even worse but their spirits are buoyed by news that James was recovering and would be back with them soon. Jeremy & Richard eventually find a tarmac road near Palmyra and decide to change their tactics: rather than disguising their cars, they disguise themselves instead. They meet James at the hospital dressed in burqas and head off towards Damascus. However, their efforts are in vain – because word has spread that they are in the country and they find a welcoming party waiting for them at their hotel.

The next day, the boys cross into Jordan and arrive at Jerash, where they invent the sport of "Old Testament NASCAR", racing their cars around a two thousand year old chariot racing circuit. Soon after, they successfully cross into Israel and make a slight detour to visit the Sea of Galilee. Once they arrive, Jeremy removes James' head bandage and says "you are healed" – he then removes his own arm bandage and says there is no evidence that there was ever a bite at all. The next morning Jeremy cooks breakfast however there were only 2 pieces of fish. Richard doesn't like fish which meant Jeremy had enough food to feed everyone, and shortly after he tried to walk on water. Before Jeremy tried to part the waters, they decided to move on. They get closer to Bethlehem and on the Mount of Olives, overlooking Jerusalem, they pull up to discuss who had the best car. James went first and declared his hatred of the automatic transmission in his Z3, he explains – "There is a place reserved in hell for the man who put that gearbox in that car. It's the ratios, it's a case of many are called but few are chosen. And many who are first shall be fourth, and if third you will actually kick down into second". James therefore selects Richard's Fiat as the car he would choose. Jeremy also chooses the Fiat, simply because he did not develop an attachment to his MX5. To him the MX5 was still a machine. Funnily enough, out of the 3 the Fiat also turned out to be the most reliable.

That night they finally make it to Bethlehem, where they arrive at a nativity scene with some gifts they purchased in Syria: James with a gold-relief medallion, Richard with a bottle of hotel shampoo labeled frankincense and Jeremy with a Nintendo DS because he couldn't find any myrrh. They peel back the covers on the manger to discover that the baby Jesus is actually a baby Stig.

Ferrari 599 GTO

Jeremy explains the history of arguably one of the best Ferrari's ever produced... the 250 GTO. Just 36 were produced, and that coupled with its road racing credentials makes it extremely rare and expensive. Jeremy stands beside one on the track and explains further, "Because the aluminium body panels were hand beaten over pieces of wood, none of them were quite the same. On this particular example for instance, the driver's door is a centimetre longer than the passenger door." The 3.0L V12 engines were all different as well, supposedly producing 295bhp, with some producing less and some more. But all of them would do 175 mph. Jeremy continues to look longingly at the car, but there is a problem. "I wish almost more than anything, I could get into this now and take it for a drive. But even though Top Gear is made by one of the world's largest and richest broadcasting organisations, we simply cannot afford the insurance." He can however, drive the 288 GTO. The 288 was also built to be a road racer, however the series it was designed for folded before it even got a chance to enter. Due to the lack of racing heritage, you can buy one for as little as £400,000. The last 288 GTO rolled off the production line in 1987, leaving the GTO name dormant... until now.

Jeremy then introduces us to the new Ferrari 599 GTO, a £300,000 road car. Jeremy is worried about this, "So they've used the GTO name on a road car. That's brave. That's like calling your infant son 'Jesus'. You need to be fairly sure he's gonna grow up to be something special. Not a burglar." Jeremy turns the traction control off to see what's what, despite the fact the track is soaking wet. After some very delicate throttle work, Jeremy still struggles to drive it quickly without spinning. The 599 GTO has a 6.0L V12 which develops 661bhp, which is an insane amount of power to put into a stripped out track style car. Jeremy suggests once you respect this power, and leave the traction control on, the results are very different. It'll do 0 – 60mph in 3.3 seconds and go on to a top speed of 208mph. The 599 GTO also has a unique feature when you are under brakes. The downshift paddle can be held, to make the on board computer downshift through the gears at exactly the right RPM. The sheer amount of electronic aids in the 599 GTO makes Jeremy feel detached from the whole experience. He feels that he is just a "big lump of meat that's come along for the ride". He continues with his biggest criticism of the car – "They called it a 'GTO'. But it was not designed for racing, so it's not a GTO. It's just a limited edition tweaked version, of the car Gordon Ramsay drives." Back in the studio, we watch the Stig take the 599 GTO for a lap of the track. It returns a time of 1:19.80. This is 0.70 slower than the Ferrari 458 Italia.

Albania

Tonight's episode begins with the TG boys in Albania, testing 3 candidate cars for the Albanian Mafia. On the ferry from Kofu to Albania, James introduces us to the car he has brought along – the new £200,000 Rolls Royce Ghost. Richard has chosen the Mercedes S65 AMG and Jeremy, well, he was meant to be in a Bentley Mulsanne. Except he wasn't – just a few days prior Bentley decided they weren't going to lend him the car. After the ferry docked in Albania, Jeremy shows us the substitute car he has arranged to use instead – a Yugo 101 Skala 55. Jeremy argues that it is similar to the Bentley in a number of ways "The Yugo is exactly the same as the Bentley Mulsanne in the same way that Roy Hattersley is the same as a tub of lard." Jeremy and Richard agree and they all hit the road, heading inland and into the rain to begin the test. James loves the Ghost, despite it being based on a BMW 7-series. Richard also loves the S65 AMG and is impressed by how much power it has for a large car. Jeremy on the other hand, isn't so kind about his "Bentley". He explains, "I must say I am terribly disappointed by the Bentley. It is the most expensive of the three – £220,000 – and from where I'm sitting, it is hard to see why."

fter a while the road turned to dirt – and instead of white lines to divide the lanes, the Albanians use large rocks instead. James and Richard both report that their cars pass smoothly over the rutted terrain – however Jeremy wasn't getting on too well in the "Bentley", eventually getting stuck on a large rock. Soon after, the road comes to an end at a river crossing – which the boys must cross on an old ferry. The boys gently load the cars, despite Jeremy's worries of the 2.8t "Bentley" sinking the boat. A little bit further down the road, it becomes apparent that there are an insane amount of Mercedes-Benz cars on the road in Albania – giving Richard's car the advantage of being able to blend in with the crowd. Jeremy reveals that they make up a whopping 80% of all cars registered in the country, and also suggesting that the majority of them have been stolen from neighbouring countries. The rain subsides and the boys hit a coast road. Jeremy's "Bentley" overheats after some spirited driving and comes to a stop on a steep hill. After cooling down it fails to start again, so he attempts to roll backwards and push start the car in reverse – but this fails as well after he runs up against a side barrier. A roadside mechanic gets it going again and the boys press on, eventually arriving at a disused submarine base – with Jeremy insisting on stopping to check out some of the rusty old subs. In the next test, the boys compare the cars to see which one is best at fitting a dead body in the boot. James goes first and attempts to lift the rather large man's body into the boot, but to no avail. Embarrassingly, the man springs back to life to help him out – climbing into the boot of the Ghost and fitting successfully. The Mercedes was up next, but a boot mounted fridge prevented the man from getting his legs in. He did however fit in the "Bentley", but he could easily be seen through the rear window – defeating the purpose of putting him in there in the first place.

The trio then line their cars up on a disused runway to have a drag race. Richard is confident that the 604bhp Mercedes will be victorious – and while James' Rolls Royce has only 563bhp, it has 3 extra gears, bringing the total to 8. Jeremy's "Bentley" fails to start so Richard and James give him a push start. It splutters to life and Jeremy leaves them behind to get a head start. Jeremy and Richard rush back to their cars and set off in pursuit – with the Mercedes being the slightly faster of the two. They soon overtake Jeremy and Richard wins the race by a few car lengths. Afterwards, the boys explore the airfield and discover a large amount of abandoned MIG fighter jets after the "Bentley" overheats. Jeremy and James re-live their cold war fantasies while the Bentley's engine cools, with Richard choosing to wait in the Mercedes.

In the final test, the boys decide to rob a bank to see which of the three makes a better getaway car. The next day, Jeremy exits the bank first and takes the Mercedes. Richard comes out next and takes the Rolls Royce – unfortunately leaving James with the "Bentley". Jeremy and Richard race through the city together and are followed closely by the Albanian Rozzers as they attempt to make their way to the ferry to Kofu. James has the heat all over him as the "Bentley" struggles to pull away. Richard and James eventually make it to the ferry and it leaves the port. James however, was not so lucky and ends up sending the Yugo over the edge of a cliff, crashing down in the valley below.

Pagani Zonda R

Jeremy tests the final Pagani Zonda - the Zonda R. The Zonda R is a confusing car that looks like a purebred racer, but it can't be raced on any tracks because it fails to meet regulations. It also can't be used on the road due to its slick tyres and the absence of indicators. The Zonda R has a 6.0L Mercedes V12 which produces 740bhp and can do 0-60mph in just 3 seconds. The top speed remains unknown, with Jeremy suggesting it is "definitely more than 230mph." Jeremy claims the R is the easiest Zonda yet to drive, due to the grippy slick tyres and the sheer stopping power available from the carbon brakes, which can take the car from 125mph to 0 in just 4.3 seconds. The R is the first Zonda to have a flappy paddle gearbox which helps you stay on the power. Jeremy continues, "This car is fantastic. An extraordinary example of what can be done when there are no rules." But at £1.46 million it is very expensive for a car which you can use almost nowhere. Jeremy sums it up, "It seems a shame then that we wave goodbye to the Zonda with a car that is absolutely brilliant, but also completely useless."

NASA's Space Exploration Vehicle

James heads to the USA to check out NASA's new Moon Buggy. The original Moon Rover (or "Buggy") cost £25,000,000 in 1971 – back when a Jaguar E-Type cost £3,500. The Moon Buggy meant that astronauts could explore more areas of the moon and generally get a better understanding of where the universe may have come from. In 1972 the Moon missions were scrapped, meaning that for the last 39 years the only Moon Buggy you could see was in a museum. Until now – the new Moon Buggy Mk II. James gets behind the wheel and takes it for a spin around the grounds at NASA. The Mk II version has a top speed of just 10mph. While James is alone in it, he was being tailed by some NASA heavies who could remotely shut it down if he did anything stupid – since it cost $4,500,000 to build. The Moon buggy has 6 motors which power 6 pairs of wheels – each can be turned individually or even raised and lowered (automatically via sensors and computer control) to pass over rough terrain. The new buggy even has sleeping quarters and a built-in toilet. It also features a unique exit system where you climb out into the suit directly and then detach from the buggy. James sums up this amazing machine, "This is the most fabulous vehicle I've ever drive, ever. But there is a problem with it – not a technical problem. It's The President. He's canceled all the funding for the next moon mission." It seems that this new Buggy will never make it to the moon at all.

Series 17

The seventeenth series of Top Gear began on BBC Two and BBC HD, on the 26th of June 2011.

Episode	Reviews	Challenges	Star in a Reasonably Priced Car
1 26/06/2011	Marauder • BMW 1 Series M Coupe • Mini John Cooper Works WRC with Amy Williams	50th Birthday of the Jaguar E-Type • Hummer alternatives in South Africa	1:56.3 – Alice Cooper (wet + automatic)
2 03/07/2011	Aston Martin Virage	High-performance hatchbacks in Lucca and around the Monaco Grand Prix track: (Citroën DS3 Racing • Fiat 500C Abarth • Renault Sport Clio 200 Cup)	1:43.5 – Ross Noble

3 10/07/2011	Second-hand bargains for the price of the Nissan Pixo (Mercedes CL600 & BMW 850Ci)	Examine toughness of the Range Rover Evoque in Las Vegas • McLaren MP4-12C vs Ferrari 458 Italia.	1:44 - Sebastian Vettel
4 17/07/2011	None	Make a train out of a specially modified car and caravans as carriages. • Jeremy Clarkson compares the Jaguar XKR-S against the Nissan GT-R	1:42.2 – Rowan Atkinson
5 24/07/2011	Lotus T125 • Jensen Interceptor	Demolish a house with second-hand military equipment Bob Geldofvs demolition experts	1:48.1 – Bob Geldof
6 31/07/2011	Electric cars for the seaside: (Nissan Leaf • Peugeot iOn)	Lamborghini Aventador • Extraordinary rally team of amputee military veterans	1:47.7 – Louis Walsh

Marauder

The first episode of Top Gear Series 17 begins with Richard Hammond in South Africa, looking at a car which makes the Hummer look like a small hatchback... the Marauder armored car. The Marauder is built in South Africa and is 21 feet long, 9 feet high and weighs in at 10 tonnes, meaning it stands out just a little bit in traffic. Richard drives around the city and describes the feeling as "Weird, because I'm both worried about bumping into things because it's big, and not worried about bumping into things because frankly who cares". The Marauder is a military spec vehicle which normal civilians can buy, provided you pass a background check to make sure you aren't associated with any terrorist organisations, and can come up with a cheque for £300,000.The Marauder is quite capable off road, climbing steep hills and controlling its weight with ease. The Marauder may only have 290bhp and a top speed of 70mph, but the sheer weight of the car means that very little can stop it. Metal fences, brick walls and even a police tow truck aren't enough. The rolling diameter of the tyres is also very big, meaning it can easily drive directly over normal family sedans, crushing them flat. Richard wreaks havoc around Johannesburg a while longer before taking the Marauder to an open field for a test, how would it stack up against a Hummer, if both cars had a 7 pound plastic explosive charge detonated under them? The Hummer went first... and was blown into thousands of unrecognisable parts. The Marauder went next... the car was so solid that the explosion was directed downwards and blew the ground away. Richard demonstrates the strength of the car by jumping in and driving the car away.

McLaren MP4-12C

The episode begins with Jeremy looking at the all new, all British McLaren MP4-12C, out on the Top Gear Test Track. Inevitably, the MP4-12C will be compared to the Ferrari 458 Italia, which most people will agree is the supercar of the moment. "McLaren themselves admit that the 458 is a great car. But they say that scientifically and mathematically, they can prove that in every single measurable way, their new car is better" says Jeremy as he goes for a drive.

At £168,000, the McLaren is less expensive than the Ferrari, it is also a little bit kinder to the environment, a little bit lighter, a tiny bit more economical, but it's also a lot more powerful. The McLaren built twin-turbo 3.8L V8 engine churns out 592bhp, compared to the Ferrari's 562bhp. It will also get from 0-60mph in 3.1 seconds and go on to a top speed of 205mph, the Ferrari is close in both regards, but none the less slower. In the bends, the McLaren feels more stable and will stick to the road when going around a corner at such a speed that would cause the Ferrari's rear end to step out, Jeremy says "This car grips on to the road, like a terrified toddler grips onto its mother's hand". One of the reasons the MP4 is so fast, is due to the traction control system, which lets you throw the car around, even in the wet, without letting you kill yourself. The MP4 also has an air brake which pops up under hard braking, and the anti-roll bars in the suspension have been replaced with computer controlled struts, the enable all four wheels to be truly independent from each other, making for better cornering and a better ride. Along with the comfortable ride, Jeremy praises the simple elegance of the interior. In every way scientific way then, the MP4 is better than a 458 – but Jeremy feels that there is something missing – it has no "zing". In part, this is due to the focused nature of the McLaren factory "it is like a science lab – serious, quiet and ordered". Jeremy continues, "You sense this lack of joy, when you're behind the wheel", likening it to operating a high tech surgical tool. He then sums the car up – "The McLaren then, is like a pair of tights – very practical and very sensible. The Ferrari though, that is a pair of stockings". Back in the studio, we watch the Stig take the MP4 for a lap – it returns a staggering 1:16.20. James puts this down to the fact that it was developed at the Top Gear Test Track, and not the Nurburgring.

Lamborghini Aventador

The final episode for Series 17 begins with Richard looking at the latest Lamborghini – the Aventador. Lamborghini is a car company that doesn't like to be rushed. Four of their previous V12 flagship models… the Miura, Countach, Diablo and the Murciélago, span some 50 years. Now there is the £248,000 Aventador, a car which Lamborghini say has more of an emphasis on handling, rather than sheer top speed like their older cars. Richard lines the car up on the run way and launches it from 0-60mph in 2.9 seconds, eventually getting up to just over 300kph (186mph) before having to break for the end of the runway. Richard tries to calm himself and quips "If that's them giving top speed a low priority, bring it on!" Given enough space, the Aventador can reach 217mph which is faster than the old Murciélago. These impressive figures come courtesy of an all-new 6.5L 691bhp V12 – an impressive feat in itself, when you realise most car companies are downsizing their engines while still attempting to increase power. The power is fed to all four wheels via a lightweight flappy paddle gearbox that can shift gears in less than 50ms. Richard selects "Corsa" mode from the on-board computer and then sets about finding out how the car handles. He soon discovers that the Aventador is extremely stable through the bends thanks to F1 style push-rod suspension and the sheer amount of grip available. It is all sounding rather good, but Richard feels that the car has lost the very thing that makes Lamborghini's of old feel special – the fear factor. It may look a bit mental, but it is a very serious car. The noise it makes is not deafening, the chassis is made from carbon fibre instead of iron and the air-conditioning works – the old Lamborghini feeling of fear and excitement whilst you drive it. Back in the studio, we watch the Stig take the Aventador for a lap – and returns a stunning time of 1:16.50.

Series 18

The eighteenth series of Top Gear began on BBC Two and BBC HD, on the 29th of January 2012, preceded by a Christmas special on 28 December 2011. One segment that was due to appear in the series, which featured May driving a jet plane around the test track, was not broadcast for unknown reasons, although it appeared in the Challenges 6 DVD and it showed it would have been part of the Saab feature in the series.

Episode	Reviews	Challenges	Star in a Reasonably Priced Car
India 28/12/2011	None	India Special Dabbawala delivery in Mumbai, motorsporting in Jaipur, and trade fair in Delhi: (Jaguar XJS • Rolls-Royce Silver Shadow • Mini Cooper)	None
1 29/01/2012	None	"Supercars Across Italy": (Lamborghini Aventador • McLaren MP4-12C • Noble M600)	1:49.4 – will.i.am (wet) (automatic)
2	Mercedes-Benz SLS AMG	Jeremy and James examine China's car industry in	1:42.1 – Matt LeBlanc

05/02/2012	Roadster	Beijing • Richard learns about NASCAR racing in Texas	
3 12/02/2012	Vauxhall Corsa VXR Nurburgring • Fiat Panda	Creating the climactic car chase for The Sweeney(Jaguar XFR • Ford Focus)	1:43.7 – Ryan Reynolds
4 19/02/2012	Ferrari FF • Bentley Continental V8 • Fisker Karma	Build and test off-road mobility scooters on the countryside	1:42.8 – Michael Fassbender (ice on the second-to-last corner)
5 26/02/2012	Maserati GranTurismo MC Stradale • Mercedes-Benz C63 AMG Coupe Black Series	Retrospective on Swedish car maker Saab • Rally-spec Škoda vs jet-powered flying man.	1:45.2 – Alex James
6 04/03/2012	"Aero-engined" Bentley, Brutus	Three stripped track cars in Donington: (KTM X-Bow • Morgan Three Wheeler • Caterham R500)	1:43.7 – Matt Smith

7 11/03/2012	BMW M5	Can you go motor racing for less than it costs to play golf? • James's childhood dream car: Ferrari 250 GT California.	1:49.8 – Slash (wet) 1:46.1 - Kimi Räikkönen

Top Gear India Special

This special episode of Top Gear begins with the boys outside of Number 10 Downing Street – where they reveal the PM, David Cameron, personally dismissed their suggestion to run a British trade mission to India, in an effort to increase business between the two countries. Top Gear ignores Mr. Cameron anyway and the boys each purchase a British car for under £7,000 and begin their journey to India.

Upon arriving, the boys meet up in the city of Bombay to see what cars the others had bought. James arrives first in a Rolls Royce Silver Shadow – a car hand wrought in Britain during the 1970's, using the very finest British car making materials. Jeremy turns up next in a Jaguar XJS – a car notorious for being utterly unreliable due to cheap electrical connectors and relays. Richard rolls up last in one of the last Mini Cooper Sports' ever made – it looks immaculate and proudly displays the Union Jack on the roof. The boys argue about which car is best, and for good reason – ahead lay a 1,300 mile journey across India and up into the Himalayas

The boys head out into the streets of Bombay to get to know their cars. Richard loves the "chunky" power produced from the Mini's tiny engine, whilst simultaneously wincing in pain from the car's rough ride, thanks to its lowered suspension. Jeremy feels extremely confident inside the XJS, all the dials are reading as they should, the engine is smooth and every single electric item in the car works. James agrees the 210bhp available in the Rolls is "adequate" and is happy to report that the car has no faults whatsoever. For their first challenge, the boys take on a mission of revolutionising the Indian "Dabbawala's" – a group of people who deliver hot, home cooked meals from housewives, directly to their husbands at work. Despite over 200,000 tins being delivered every day – only 1 mistake is made for every 6,000,000 deliveries. Rather than delivering the tins by train, the boys decide to deliver them by car to help bring the efficiency up to 100%. Put simply, they fail miserably due to spilt tins and a slow delivery due to traffic jams.

After their dismal failure, the boys have to head north to the city of Jaipur – however instead of driving, the producer decides to put them on an overnight train. The cars are loaded and James queues to buy the tickets – with Jeremy and Richard going to have lunch instead. Over lunch, Jeremy gives Richard a present – in the form of a massive bass guitar. They discuss the idea of having a trade party once they arrive in Delhi and perhaps even resurrecting the Top Gear Band. They purchase a drum kit and a keyboard and then board the train to Jaipur. During the trip, Top Gear's producer Andy Wilman is roped in to do the vocals – and they hold a practice session much to the dismay of the other passengers. Later on, the boys decide to hang large banners down the side of the train to help advertise Britain as it travels across the country. The banners are created and Jeremy attempts to feed it out one of the side doors, along the side of the carriage – it gets caught on something and is ripped clean out of his hands. At the next stop, the banners are successfully put in place the train continues on – without James. At Jaipur station, the boys disembark and the train splits – causing the banners to break in half and change their message completely.

Upon unloading the cars, Jeremy and Richard discover that the air-conditioning in the Rolls is actually fully functional – and they proceed to drain the refrigeration gas before he catches up with them all. Outside of Jaipur, the boys find a nice 1 kilometer section of road in the hills, and hold a traditional British Hill Climb event. A group of locals turn up with a selection of vehicles and post their own times on the course – before the boys each have a go. Richard and James hold back, so they didn't decimate the local's times. Jeremy however, went flat out and ended up winning the event. Afterwards, they all split up and decorate their own cars. Richard paints the flag of Mexico on the Mini's bonnet, Jeremy applies floral wallpaper and a boot mounted toilet to his Jaguar – and James fits British and Indian flags along with floral arrangements to his Rolls. The boys then head north to Delhi, to hold their ambassadorial party. The roads are among the most dangerous in the world – and night fell when there was still 80 miles to go until the overnight stopover point. After a nervous 2 hours, they arrive.

The next morning, the road chaos continued – with the only difference being that you could now see what was about to kill you. Eventually they arrive in Delhi and begin to set up the party – which doesn't go well. The following day, the boys modify their cars further – to prepare them for the journey north into the Himalayas. Jeremy fits chunky off road tyres on his Jaguar, along with open exhaust headers which exit vertically out of the bonnet. James also fitted off road tyres to the Rolls, as did Richard with his Mini – along with a front mounted winch. Jeremy an James argue for an hour about who ruined their car more – before stopping and swapping cars to compare. Jeremy only lasts a few minutes in the Rolls before asking to swap back. Eventually they begin the ascent into the Himalayas and finally find a bit of peace and quiet is found – well until Jeremy rolls through in his Jaguar running an open exhaust. After passing Shimla, the roads turn from bad to worse – and eventually the tarmac disappears all together. The front of Richard's mini gets ripped off after an attempt to pull James' Rolls up a steep incline – which later forces the boys to stop early and camp for the night due to him having no headlights.

The next day, Richard mends the Mini whilst Jeremy moans about his poor night's sleep. After a brief game of Straight Six Cricket, Jeremy, Richard and James reach the Chinese border and have the cars put on giant plinths by the roadside. Jeremy sums up the gesture. "The Mini, the Jag and the Rolls would be mounted on plinths, here, high in the mountains, by the road connecting India and China. So that forevermore people traveling between these two great economic superpowers will be reminded that far away there's a smile island called Britain. Great Britain."

Jeremy mentions in a later episode that the three cars they left on plinths in India, in fact had to be moved because they were situated on top of an ancient burial ground.

If you are in the market for a mid-engined supercar but not interested in a Ferrari 458 Italia – which one is best for you?

None of the team can agree on an answer – so they each choose a car and reconvene in Lecce, Italy, to try to settle their differences.

James arrives first in the McLaren MP4-12C. A car which James says is made with an "almost psychotic" attention to detail, rather like him. Jeremy arrives next in a car which is also very like him, the very loud and shouty Lamborghini Aventador. Richard turns up in a Noble M600 and is immediately set upon by the other two presenters who criticise the M600 for having an engine from a Volvo XC90, or that it was made on a light industrial estate in Leicestershire. Richard argues that the M600's power to weight ratio will more than make up for this. All three jump in their cars and hit the highway where they are each bowled over by the sheer amount of power offered by each car. Half an hour later, they all pull into a service station and brim the tanks in each car as they receive their first a challenge. It is revealed that they will all travel to the Nardo Test Track, where they will compete against each other to see who can post the highest top speed.

The Nardo Test Track is an 8 mile circle of tarmac which is so vast it can be seen from space... it is simply one endless corner. Lamborghini and McLaren had both sent a team of technicians to ensure that their cars were in top shape for the challenge with Richard on his own because no-one from Noble turned up. Accurate speedometers were fitted to each car and the boys were sent out. On the sighting lap, the boys each put the case forward on why their car will win. Richard feels confident, and says "My car is the fastest with a top speed of 225mph. Jeremy's Lambo 217mph. James' McLaren 205mph – or to put it another way, walking pace". The boys put some space between each other and then go for it. After a few nerve racking laps at full throttle, they all reach their top speeds and reconvene back at the pits. It is revealed that Richard had the biggest testes with a top speed of 204.8mph in the M600. Jeremy came second with 204.3mph in the Lambo, and James last with 201.6mph in the McLaren.

It is later revealed that on the top speed test, the Lambo did 7mpg, the McLaren did 8mpg, and the Noble managed 9mpg – making it not only the fastest, but also the most economical. Next, the boys drive north to Rome. Richard is still smug from the previous day's victory and shows off the Noble M600's turbo flutter as he passes Jeremy and James. However his gloating is short lived as the gearbox repeatedly crunches as he tries to engage a gear, and he is forced to pull over onto the hard shoulder. The Noble clearly isn't going anywhere, so Jeremy and James leave him to it. As the cars ate up the miles, they both begin to know them better. James has fallen in love with the McLaren's clever technologies. Jeremy marvels at how easy the Aventador is to drive, compared to Lamborghini's of old. Richard on the other hand, finally has a tow truck arrive after a 2.5 hour wait. Meanwhile, Jeremy and James are pulled over by the police as it turns out it is a public holiday in Italy and it is illegal to be actually working without a permit. They continue on to Rome for dinner and then meet up with Richard after lunch time the next day Richard is now driving a different coloured car. It turns out the original M600's clutch disintegrated and damaged the gearbox so a man from Noble drove a new car out overnight from Britain.

"Three days ago if you'd said to me, which would you rather have... I would have said the Ferrari. I mean, it's the obvious choice. But now... no. I'd have this. I know a Ferrari 458 is just a technical masterpiece and it looks wonderful, but this has got something the Ferrari doesn't have. It has a character. It's like a big daft orange dog", Jeremy says.

Richard continues, "It's won me over, completely. It's not just the best car here, it is better than the Ferrari 458, for me it is one of the best cars in the world right now. I absolutely love it."

With two votes against the Ferrari, what does James think? Well, "This is brilliant. I've really grown to like it – and let's not forget its £35,000 or so cheaper than the Ferrari 458 and that is a huge amount of money… but the Ferrari still gives me more fizz."

The boys reach their destination at the Imola circuit, where they receive their next challenge. The boys must each lap the circuit and attempt to beat the time set by the Ferrari 458 at the hands of the Stig's Italian cousin. Italian Stig jumps in the 458 and sets a cracking time of 1:56.60. The boys each jump in their car and go out for a practice session, to see how their cars perform on a track. Jeremy admires the Aventador's 4wd system and fade-free carbon bakes. Richard on the other hand, has no driver aids to help him out and instead has to concentrate on driving smoothly. Someone who does have a lot of driver aids, is James in the McLaren but he was concentrating on memorising the track layout instead. At the end of the day, the boys knew the track but still felt daunted by the challenge which lay ahead.

Imola is one of the most dangerous tracks on earth, as Jeremy explains. "Its narrow, fast and ringed with unforgiving walls and trees. Gilles Villeneuve, Gerhard Berger, Nelson Pike, Riccardo Patrese, Rubens Barrichello… at some point in history every corner here has claimed the ego of a big name and some corners have claimed even more than that. After Senna's death in 1994, changes were made to the track to slow the cars down, but even so, if we were going to beat that Ferrari, we'd still be going through the first bend at nearly 200mph."

The next morning, the boys hit the track and progressively reduce their times as they push just a little bit harder each lap. Jeremy leans on the brakes harder each time, as he becomes more confident in the sheer stopping power available. James places more trust in the McLaren's driver aids, while Richard tries to carry as much speed as possible through the bends and ends up going off the track at high speed whilst narrowly avoiding a spin. They all push on and after a short rest stop, go out one last time to try and improve on their times.

Back in the studio, the final lap times are revealed. Richard managed a 2:03.30 second lap. James did a slower 2:06.40. With Jeremy winning the challenge with a time of 1:59.10. Unfortunately, all were slower than the Stig's lap of 1:56.60 in the Ferrari 458.

Series 19

The nineteenth series of Top Gear began on BBC Two and BBC HD, on the 27th of January, 2013

Episode	Reviews	Challenges	*Star in a Reasonably Priced Car*
1 27/01/2013	Pagani Huayra	Take the Bentley Continental GT Speed to a Welsh Rally stage. • Build a car smaller than a Peel P50 (Jeremy's "P45")	2:09.1 – Damian Lewis (snow)
2 03/02/2013	None	Supercar road trip from Las Vegas, Nevada to Calexico, California: (Lexus LFA • SRT Viper • Aston Martin Vanquish)	1:45.4 – Mick Fleetwood
3 10/02/2013	Toyota GT86	Epic race from Wembley to the San Siro stadium in Milan: Shelby Mustang GT500 vs. the pan-European rail network	1:44.4 – Amy Macdonald

4 17/02/2013	Mastretta MXT in Mexico • Hot hatchbacks: (Ford Focus ST • Renault Megane RenaultSport Cup 265 • Vauxhall Astra VXR)	Rugby match with Kia Cee'ds	1:42.9 – Lewis Hamilton
5 24/02/2013	None	Jeremy and Richard Design a vehicle for the elderly ("Rover James"/Fiat Multipla) in Christchurch • Range Rover vs an autonomous military machine	1:43.6 – James McAvoy
6 03/03/2013	None	Find source of the Nile: (BMW 5-Series Touring • Volvo 850R Estate • Subaru Impreza WRX Sport Estate)	None
7 10/03/2013	None	Find source of the Nile: (BMW 5-Series Touring • Volvo 850R Estate • Subaru Impreza WRX Sport Estate)	None

Supercar Roadtrip: Nevada to Calexico

In another challenge, the presenters picked three super cars to take on an epic road trip. Since it was Hammond's turn to select the challenge location, the team went to the Western United States. Jeremy selected the Lexus LFA, James chose the new Aston Martin Vanquish, and Richard took the SRT Viper. After a brief drive in the Nevada desert, the trio headed to Las Vegas Motor Speedway, specifically the drag strip, to compete in drag races organised by the Las Vegas Police Department; whom organised it with the theory that allowing people to drag race, legally, at a closed circuit, would prevent street racing. Despite the high performance of their cars, the trio were beaten by modified production cars, and 4WD cars, in each of their drag races.

The boys leave Las Vegas. James and Richard make fun of Jeremy's LFA for lacking not only Bluetooth connection and iPod connectors, but cup holders, despite being the most expensive car. They are then tasked to head to Willow Springs International Motorsports Park, but, along the way, they stop on a grooved road, where each car drives over the grooves and produces the notes to the "William Tell Overture." The trio considers the road "annoying and out of tune". When they reach Willow Springs, they are forced to play an aerial version of Laser Quest, where they would drive 5 laps around the track, whilst being chased by two Aermacchi SF.260 armed with laser guns. In the end, James won the challenge by being hit only 17 times.

The boys then head for Los Angeles, California. In order to do "real world" testing, Richard devised a challenge to see who could burn the best elevens and do the best donuts. The three instead ended up drawing a phallus and left LA. The team then stayed for a night in Palm Springs. However, the producers gave them a final challenge. The three would drive from Palm Springs to the Mexican border at Calexico the following morning, and the last to make it to the Mexican border would have to travel into the country itself to drive the Mastretta MXT, a Mexican sports car made fun of by the presenters in an earlier series, for a later segment on the show. In revenge for taking them to America, Jeremy and James sabotaged Hammond's Viper, causing him to lose 10 minutes in the race. Despite making a stop for fuel, Jeremy made it to the finish line first, with James in second. Richard then walked to the border being the last person to arrive. At the studio, James and Jeremy end by saying that the Viper was awful and that the Vanquish and LFA were amazing.

Source of the River Nile

This two-episode Special takes place in Africa. The episode was shot in 2012.

The trio are told to buy three used estate cars for up to £1,500 in Britain and report at a small village in rural Uganda. Jeremy arrives in a BMW 528i Touring, Richard in a Subaru Impreza WRX Estate and James in a Volvo 850R Wagon. Their challenge is revealed once they arrived: to find the true source of the river Nile.

They set off, and discover that exploring isn't as difficult as first thought when they go on a nice easy drive and find Lake Victoria, of whom the Victorian Explorers thought was the source of the Nile. However, once there, they are then told that it is not the actual source of the Nile and there were two other disputed locations for it, one in Rwanda and one in Burundi. However, Jeremy Clarkson insists that both of these locations are wrong and decides they should head west towards Lake Edward to see whether there is a river that links it from Lake Kivu in Rwanda; which Jeremy believes is the source.

In their journey west, they stop to visit the Entebbe Airport, scene of an important hostage rescue by Israeli Specialist, and discover that their back-up car for the trip is a Ford Scorpio Estate. They continue into Kampala, Uganda's capital city where they get held up in a traffic jam overnight, finding it to be some of the most horrendous traffic they'd ever seen; while still stuck in it in the morning the trio buy breakfast from local vendors.

Once out of the jam, they continue on well-maintained highways west, finding their trip incredibly easy before reaching the town of Mbarara in the southwest of the country, via a stop in Jezza, a village in Mpigi District (where Richard is given a present), after driving through tea plantations in an attempt to discover a lovely teahouse hotel, which in the mind of Richard, was bound to be found due to the tea programs he'd seen.

In Mbarara they stay in a shabby, filthy hotel, with Jeremy having a bed with faeces on it. Next morning, disgusted, they leave the hotel; whereupon, Richard has the idea (in an effort to make up for the trouble) to make their cars into 'mobile campers'. Each go out to find what they want and change their estates. James modifies his Volvo by adding a library and a workshop (which Jeremy admits was a smart idea); Richard adds a stove, sink, and cupboards; and Jeremy adds a coffin and a fridge mainly for beer along with attachments to the side for a portable bathroom. The coffin he uses to put his clothes in, while he would be sleeping on "Egyptian cotton and duck down."

They leave for Lake Edward, camping overnight there because of its beauty before heading in search of the river heading for Lake Kivu. While James suffers problems and is left behind to sort it out, Richard and Jeremy check the rivers flowing into the lake, only to find none of the rivers connect the two lakes as they all flow in the wrong direction. This destroys Jeremy's theory, and so that night, he checks the map and devises a new one; he believes that the source of the Nile must be on the other side of Lake Victoria. His reasoning is that the Mediterranean Sea is effectively an inland sea and so Gibraltar is the true mouth of the Nile, rather than Alexandria in Egypt making him believe the source is somewhere around the east side of the lake.

After discovering this, they decide that they must drive straight to the other side of Lake Victoria to get to the southeast coast in Tanzania near the Serengeti. They start this journey by heading south into the Rwenzori Mountains, finding the going hard and most of the time getting their vehicles stuck in mud; James' Volvo, which had lost its protective skid plate, is fixed by using a piece of metal from the passenger door of Jeremy's BMW, something he later discovers and accuses him of theft; in addition to this, Jeremy's estate is also struck by a falling branch, which cracks the windscreen. His car suffers worst from the mud, while Richard has it easier.

After spending the night in the countryside, James wakes up to find out that Jeremy has taken a piece of metal from the bonnet of the Volvo to fix what James had done to his BMW, which leaves him in a bad mood; not because he took it but because he did a shoddy job of it. As well as "fixing" his car, Jeremy attaches a log to the back of his BMW to make braking and hill starts better. However, although it works, this backfires when the log, which is left loose, bounces up and shatters his rear window.

After driving across Rwanda and crossing into Tanzania, both James and Jeremy find replacements for what they lost from their cars off Richard's bonnet and rear window. Richard replaces those missing bits by stealing Jeremy's toilet and placing it on the bonnet and a piece of cardboard for the rear window.

As they travel eastwards, the trio are stopped by a river and realise it is too deep to wade through with their cars, especially since there are crocodiles lurking within it. Using a flying machine with a camera Jeremy invented for the trip, they learn there is no bridge or crossing point both up-river and down-river; Jeremy therefore comes up with the idea of making their own car-ferry, designed specifically to take their cars across the river, (similar to one they had seen in Albania) using wood and rope to fashion it. Even though both Jeremy and Richard manage to get across with it but nearly get stuck at the other end, and James almost sinks the ferry with his car since the weight of it isn't evenly distributed (which the danger was further heightened when Jeremy decided to pull the ferry using his car), the trio manage to get across safely. However, when the producers tried to get the Ford Scorpio back-up car onto the ferry, the ferry wasn't secured, so the car missed it and went straight into the river, much to the three's amusement, so the trio left the producers to clean up their mess.

Upon reaching Lake Victoria, the three decide to use a proper ferry to get across it to Tanzania. When they reach the other side the next day, Richard decides to disembark at a beach and show off his 4X4 Subaru, but gets it stuck in the sand, and when trying to repay the 40 locals that helped him to get it out, he ended up losing his lunch to them. The others disembark at a proper jetty and later reunite to find the river they believe leads to the source.

While stopping for a moment, all three decide that the cars are all great, but when separate from the others, they each claim that their car is the best. Eventually, they finally find the river they were looking for and begin to follow it to the predicted source of the Nile. However, they come across a rough road they have to travel on, which Jeremy describes as a true "Car-Killer", and soon it starts to take its toll on the cars as they try to make their next camp. Jeremy's airbags has been deployed, James had several punctures and one of alloys was damaged and replaced, but Richard's car suffers the worst damage when the left wheel's rod steering, which was rusted to begin with, finally snaps apart, leaving him to try to fix it, with the back-up car no longer available. Despite usual Top Gear behaviour in such a situation, the other two, who made camp, decide to wait for Richard for a while longer the next morning before setting off. Just as that deadline is nearly reached, James and Jeremy spot their third arriving, Richard having fixed his car enough to survive the last leg.

James and Jeremy decide once Richard is back, that since only one person can be remembered for finding the source, and the other two will be forgotten, that they should have a race to find the source. At first, Jeremy decides to go slow to avoid more incidents, but soon speeds up when he realised he was getting nowhere. After many blind decisions had been made, and many wrong turns, they soon find they have to leave their cars and find the source on foot, James having to since his rear suspension had just collapsed.

Iin the end, James finds it first, which turns out to be merely a very small pond being fed from somewhere beneath large rocks, just seconds before Jeremy does, with Richard arriving a little later. The pair congratulate James, and two flags, the Top Gear one and the British Flag, are planted at the spot, with the three posing for a photo like the Victorian explorers. A caption over the photo, says "James May, Discoverer of the True Source of the Nile, and Two Other Blokes."

As the credits roll, each member of the crew, like in previous specials and such, has their name altered with each displaying their surname with "Dr." before and ", I Presume?" afterwards (such as "Dr. Clarkson, I Presume?" and so forth).

Series 20

The twentieth series of Top Gear started airing on BBC Two on Sunday the 30th of June 2013.

Episode	Reviews	Challenges	Star in a Reasonably Priced Car
1 30/06/2013	Renaultsport Clio 200 • Peugeot 208 GTi • Ford Fiesta ST • Vauxhall Astra Tech Line	AC45 Racing Yacht vs Toyota Auris • Introduction of the new Reasonably Priced Car: Vauxhall Astra	1:48.8 – Charles Dance 1:46.8 – Warwick Davis 1:48.5 – Rachel Riley 1:48.9 – Joss Stone 1:46.7 – David Haye 1:45.6 – Jimmy Carr 1:51.5 – Mike

			Rutherford 1:45.1 – Brian Johnson
2 14/07/2013	Ferrari F12 Berlinetta • BAC Mono	Best taxi • Tribute to BBC Television Centre	1:49.9 – Ron Howard
3 14/07/2013	None	Spanish road trip in "budget" convertibles: McLaren MP4-12C Spider • Audi R8 V10 Spyder • Ferrari 458 Spider	1.47.8 – Benedict Cumberbatch
4 21/07/2013	Mercedes SLS AMG Black Series • Mercedes SLS Ford Transit hovervan AMG Electric Drive	Ford Transit hovervan	1:46.1 – Hugh Jackman
5 28/07/2013	Porsche 911• Lamborghini Aventador Roadster • Lamborghini Sesto Elemento • Mazda CX-5 • Volkswagen	Best crossovers for caravanners	1:51.0 – Steven Tyler

	Tiguan		
6 04/08/2013	Jaguar F-Type • New Bus for London • Range Rover Sport	Tribute to British automobile manufacturing	1:43.1 - Mark Webber

Ferrari F12
Berlinetta2

Jeremy goes to Hertfordshire to test the Ferrari F12 Berlinetta, assessing its practicality as an everyday car. Except Jeremy wasn't in Letchworth. He was 430 miles away in Pitlochry, which is in Perth and Kinross, Scotland.

" Budget Convertibles across Spain"

The trio plan to drive across Spain to test three new "budget convertibles". Clarkson selects a bright yellow £195,000 McLaren MP4-12C Spider, Hammond takes a red £198,000 Ferrari 458 Spider, and May chooses a gray £121,000 Audi R8 V10 Spyder. Their first competition is to see who can drive through the marina area of Puerto Banus with the fewest number of pictures taken. May's R8 is snapped 22 times, Hammond's Ferrari 47 times, and Clarkson's MP4 a whopping 438 times. The next day, they come across an immense area of abandoned, newly-built flats and decide to conduct a noise test. Hammond believes that he has won when his 458 generates 107 dB of engine noise at full tilt (to 105 dB from the other two), but is declared the loser when Clarkson and May declare the object to be to generate the least amount of noise. They then set off on a curving road in the Sierra Nevada mountain range to test the limits of their cars, but their reverie is cut short, literally, when the road suddenly stops, unfinished due to lack of funds. When action switches back to the studio, they note that the R8 was also first in an (unshown) economy test.

The trio use a near-deserted motorway to head further north into Spain. Searching for a place to test the top speeds of their cars. They chance across the disused Ciudad Real Central Airport. After amusing themselves with the still-active facilities in the abandoned terminal, they give themselves permission to use the main runway to test their cars. First is a top-speed test: Clarkson's MP4 reaches 198 mph (319 km/h), besting the 458's 193 mph (311 km/h) and the R8's 186 mph (299 km/h). The next test, campaigned over a half-mile length of runway, is a race in which the presenters must start with the tops down, and finish with the tops up; the MP4 wins again, followed by the R8 and the 458. Instead of renting hotel rooms, the presenters find another series of abandoned housing projects and squat in an unoccupied house for the night.

The trio then enter Madrid and find yet another huge abandoned housing project. Commenting on the size of the project, Clarkson opines that the development would be an ideal location for a street-racing circuit, which they create and christen the "Circuito de Sir Francis Drake". Calling their event the "Madrid Grand Prix", they import the Stig to set a benchmark lap in a Jaguar XKR-S convertible. None of the presenters best the Stig's 0:57.5; Hammond runs a 0:58.5, followed by Clarkson's 0:59.1 and May's 1:00.8. Back at the studio, Clarkson claims that the MP4 has won, while May produces a chart demonstrating how the R8 has won. In the end, though, all three presenters decide that they would rather have the Ferrari.

Mercedes-Benz SLS Electric Drive

Jeremy compare the Mercedes SLS AMG Black Series to the Mercedes SLS AMG Electric Drive. The Black Series is now faster and has better handing than the normal one due to its lighter weight, more horsepower, a rear wing and electronic differentials. He sums the Black Series up by saying that it was built to make a lap fast, while the normal one was built to make a lap fun. The Electric Drive however, comes with a more powerful engine and its own "high-visibility jacket", although it is very quiet. But, against the petrol-powered Black Series, it is dominant in a drag race because of its four independent motors powering each wheel, despite it being heavier by half a ton, due to having 864 batteries in the spine of the chassis. Jeremy sums it up as a brilliant car, but the drawbacks are quite significant, as the range is not very good, and it cost £360,000 but it does show that when the oil runs out, cars can still develop. The Stig sets a time of 1:21;7 in the Electric Drive, but sets a faster time of 1:19:0 in the Black Series, showing the difference between the petrol and the electric versions of a car.

Lamborghini Sesto Elemento

Richard tests the new Lamborghini Aventador Roadster in Italy, then he moves onto the Lamborghini Sesto Elemento. Hammond drives it around the Imola racetrack, noting how powerful and basic the car is. The Stig then takes the Sesto Elemento around the track; he spins off the track at one point, but manages to finish a lap in 1:14.0. The car was then removed from the board, due to it not being road legal.

Series 21

The twenty-first series of Top Gear started airing on BBC Two and BBC Two HD on the 2nd of February, 2014.

Episode	Reviews	Challenges	Star in a Reasonably Priced Car
1 02/02/2014	None	Prove that the hot hatchbacks of their youth were better than their modern equivalents: (Volkswagen Golf Mk2 GTI • Vauxhall Nova SRi • Ford Fiesta XR2i)	1:50.1 – Hugh Bonneville (wet)
2 09/02/2014	Alfa Romeo 4C • Gibbs Quadski • McLaren P1	Alfa Romeo 4C vs Gibbs Quadski • James visits Camp Bastion in Afghanistan	1:49.9 – Tom Hiddleston (very wet)
3 16/02/2014	Zenvo STI	Trip through Ukraine in compact hatchbacks: (Volkswagen Up! • Ford Fiesta • Dacia Sandero)	1:49.4 – James Blunt (very, very wet)
4 23/02/	Mercedes Benz G63 AMG 6x6 • Caterham 160 •	Mercedes Benz G63 AMG 6x6	1.54.5 – Jack Whitehall (automatic)

2014	Caterham 620R • Alfa Romeo Touring Disco Volante		
5 02/03/2014	Porsche 918 • BMW M135i • VW Golf GTi Mk7 • (Mercedes-Benz A45 AMG)	Make a commercial for reducing cycle-related accidents	1:44.7 – Aaron Paul
6 09/03/2014	None	Build a bridge over the River Kwai: (Isuzu TX • Isuzu TX • Hino FB110)	None
7 16/03/2014	None	Build a bridge over the River Kwai: (Isuzu TX • Isuzu TX • Hino FB110)	None

McLaren P1

Jeremy is in the genteel surroundings of Bruges in Belgium to review the McLaren P1, which he later drives it around the Circuit de Spa-Francorchamps racetrack, noting how powerful and basic the car is.

Mercedes Benz G63 AMG 6x6

Richard travels to the United Arab Emirates in order to review the six-wheeled Mercedes Benz G63 AMG 6x6.

Porsche 918

Richard heads to the Yas Marina Circuit to review Porsche's new hybrid supercar: the 918 Spyder. He praised it for its mind-boggling straight line performance and incredible handling capabilities as well as its low emissions and great efficiency. He concluded with the statement that the McLaren P1 had used hybrid technology to liven up the supercar for today's performance enthusiasts, but that the 918 Spyder used hybrid technology not just to liven up the supercar for today, yet to also preserve it for the future in which there will be more stringent emissions and economy regulations.

Burma Special

Beginning in Rangoon (referred to often as Yangon - its modern name), the old capital city of Burma the presenters are told to meet up in the People's Square opposite the Shwedagon Pagoda. Jeremy is the first to arrive in what he dubs the 'sports lorry', a yellow Isuzu built around 1959. The next to arrive is James, in the smallest of the three, leading Jeremy to mock it as a van. James' lorry has a crane attachment on the back, which he later puts to good use. Jeremy demonstrates his speaker system to James while they wait for Richard and justifies why he is wearing a tie saying "because I am a modern lorry driver and modern lorry drivers are crisp and sharp. The days are over when you simply turned up with a glove box full of strong pornography and egg on your vest". Hammond then arrives at the Square with "a glovebox full of strong pornography and egg on his vest". Hammond's truck is mocked for its size and for being a Hindu temple by James. The presenters also critizes his seat which Jeremy likens to a church pew. Jeremy also suggest that as Hammond's lorry was originally a farm truck it was used for transporting heroin in the Golden Triangle. The presenters then formally receive their challenge. They are tasked with building a bridge that is strong enough to support the weight of their lorries over the River Kwai in Thailand.

The presenters, excited about their bridge building challenge, set off making a route through Rangoon up to Naypyidaw, across the Shan State, and finally crossing the border into Northern Thailand. On the streets of Rangoon the presenters come to grips with just how dodgy their ancient lorries are. Jeremy's gearbox is extremely difficult to change, he accidentally activates his 'tipper', Richard's discovers that none of his gauges or dials work, and James realizes that there is a significant amount of play in the steering and that his lorry has no handbrake. Despite their problems the presenters press on following James' lead in the crowded streets, Jeremy remarking on the history of Burma's rule under General Ne Win. James eventually leads them down a narrow street, down which Jeremy knocks over a lady's fruit stand. Whilst he organises payment for the Burmese shop keeper, Hammond is forced to use the crane James' truck so that he can clear a set of low wires.

Having forded rivers, climbed mountains and endured a Burmese trucker stop, they must now venture into the Shan state, an area rife with civil war and normally closed to western TV crews, as they head towards Thailand and their final challenge - to build a bridge over the River Kwai

After attending a party in the Shan State, the presenters reach what they believe is the River Kwai, where they are challenged with building a bridge over the river, which is longer than they had imagined. James plots a bridge meanwhile Hammond goes into town looking for supplies and Jeremy goes into town looking for food and other workers. Jeremy gets workers and brings back a large crane which eventually fails and tips over destroying a part of the bridge. Halfway through construction, Jeremy discovers that the river is actually River Kok. In the end the bridge is completed and each of the vehicles are driven over it, completing the challenge. During the end credits, each member of the cast and crew's first name was credited as "Sir Alec", in homage to Sir Alec Guinness, who starred in the movie, The Bridge on the River Kwai.

Series 22

The twenty-second series of Top Gear began airing on BBC Two and BBC Two HD on the 27th of December, 2014. It was soon mired in controversy following two major incidents including the attack on the presenters in Argentina while filming "The Patagonia Special", and the suspension of Clarkson and subsequent non-renewal of his contract by the BBC in the wake of his assault on a show producer. This series is the last to feature Clarkson, May, and Hammond as presenters, and the final episodes remain incomplete and unaired.

Episode	Reviews	Challenges	Star in a Reasonably Priced Car
Patagonia Special 27/12/2014	None	Drive from Bariloche to Ushuaia: (Porsche 928 GT • Lotus Esprit V8 • Ford Mustang Mach 1)	None
Patagonia Special 28/12/2014	None	Drive from Bariloche to Ushuaia: (Porsche 928 GT • Lotus Esprit V8 • Ford Mustang Mach 1)	None
1 25/01/2015	Lamborghini Huracán • Renault Twizy	Race across the urban landscape of St Petersburg	Ed Sheeran (1:54.3)

2 04/11/2007	None	Australian NT road trip in GT cars: (BMW M6 Gran Coupe • Nissan GT-R • Bentley Continental GT V8S)	Kiefer Sutherland (1:49.2)
3 8/02/2015	None	Homemade ambulance challenge: (Porsche 944 Turbo • Ford Scorpio Cardinal • Chevy G20 V8 Van)	Daniel Riccardo (1:42.2)
4 15/02/2015	BMW M3 • BMW i8 • Mercedes-AMG GT S	Hammond pays homage to the Land Rover Defender	Margot Robbie (1:47.1) Will Smith (1:47.2)
5 22/02/2015	Porsche Cayman GTS • Chevrolet Corvette Stingray • LaFerrari	James and Jeremy look at the weird and wonderful history of Peugeot	Olly Murs (1:44.2)
6 01/03/2015	Lexus RCF • Lexus LFA	Richard is dropped into British Columbia, Canada to test a watch with a built-in emergency beacon: (Chevrolet Silverado • Ford F-150 Hennessey VelociRaptor)	Gillian Anderson (1:48.5 V. Wet)

7 08/03/2015	Jaguar F-Type R • Eagle Low Drag GT • Mazda MX-5 ND	James competes in a world rallycross race alongside Tanner Foust (Top Gear USA host)	Nicholas Hoult (1:44.7)
8 Unshown	Subaru WRX STi • VW Golf R	The trio go for a drive in the countryside in classic convertibles: (Fiat 124 Spider • MGB GT • Peugeot 304 Cabriolet)	Gary Lineker (Not yet Shown)
9 Unshown	None	The trio are challenged to each purchase a second hand SUV on the cheap and see who got the best deal. Also, Clarkson is on and off the track in a trio of luxurious limousines.	Henry Cavill (Not yet Shown)

Patagonia Special

Jeremy Clarkson, Richard Hammond and James May take three V8-engined sports cars on a grueling 1600-mile journey through the spectacular landscapes of Patagonia. Along the way they encounter rough roads, collapsed bridges, broken bones and a cow as they press onwards against the odds in a quest to reach the southernmost city in the world.

The trio are challenged with finding a car with a V8 engine. Clarkson chooses a Porsche 928, which the other presenters mock for being boring. Hammond chooses a 1971 Ford Mustang Mach 1, which is berated for having a number of pointless features. James May chooses a Lotus Esprit, which is constantly belittled for its notorious history of unreliability; even James admits that it is "a risk". They are first told that they have to travel 130 miles to Butch Cassidy's final resting place, much to the shock and delight of the presenters, Jeremy in particular. On the way, they drive through Bariloche, a place Hammond describes as "a haven for Nazi war criminals". Hammond's car experiences problems at this stage; the Mach 1 has poor steering and requires a lot of fuel stops. It then breaks down a mile and a half from the destination, forcing him to push it the rest of the way.

After spending the night in the house, they are then told to drive to Ushuaia in Tierra del Fuego, the southernmost city in the world, 1600 miles away. Hammond's car breaks down a number of times which he blames on Jeremy's route. Both the Porsche and the Mustang get beached in a swamp, forcing the Lotus to rescue them, much to their surprise. They also drive over numerous dangerous bridges, one of which is very unsturdy and ends up leading them to a dead end. At this point, Jeremy notes that although it is the most unreliable car to have brought, the Lotus is surprisingly doing the best. Along the way, they notice a Citroën 2CV following them, which they realise is the comedy backup car. Clarkson notes his particular dislike for this car, saying that the only reason he got on to the original series of Top Gear was because he spent his screen-test ranting about how much he hated it for twenty minutes.

Hammond then decides to change the route, as Clarkson's had led them along numerous dangerous roads which Hammond claimed to have damaged his Mustang. Hammond's route proves to be worse, driving back over the Andes and on rickety roads. Hammond's car loses two gears, and the Porsche's window wipers bizarrely turn on without any instruction to. Jeremy cannot turn them off, and his engine breaks down numerous times. It is later revealed that damage to a shock absorber has affected the electrical systems. Hammond and May continue, and Jeremy is left with two options – to fix the car, which involves doing manual labour (something he hates) and is very complicated, or to drive in the 2CV. When the Lotus and Mustang stop, James is infuriated by Hammond's camping suggestion. Hammond returns with a cow, though James opposes this, saying they already did that joke. Despite Jeremy's incompetence, he fixes the Porsche and is also annoyed with the camping. James and Hammond annoy him further by adding garish visuals to the Porsche.

In the ensuing rant, Hammond is stripped of leadership, and the team drive on.

Continuing from the first part, the trio continue on the road. They do lap racing, though give up after Hammond's front window is smashed. They then struggle to find the road and drive to a locked gate, at which point they suggest walking to collect bolt cutters. Jeremy immediately opposes the walking and suggests they ride horses, much to the others' dismay. James then falls off and cracks three ribs, causing him to be immensely slow getting in and out of his car, and he becomes incredibly cantankerous. With the Porsche's condition poorer than ever, Jeremy decides they have proved they can survive Patagonia and should now focus on the football game. The presenters therefore modify their cars, fill them with supplies and get on a ferry to the island.

However, as the ferry cannot transport them directly due to territorial disputes between Argentina and Chile, they are dropped on a beach a mile away from the road. They struggle to overcome the beach due to the amount of boulders and the rising tide, and waste most of their supplies in the endeavor. The Lotus is trapped by the rising tide, and the team are forced to camp, although the scenery and night sky mean that for once, they are not very sorry about this. The next day, on high mountains, the Mach 1 crashes and shears a track rod. The others come to a lake which a pickup truck takes them across, though James is forced to leave behind a trailer he was using as it does not fit. Hammond repairs his car miraculously, though is forced to drive through the lake as the pickup truck has left.

They continue, only to be informed by the team that Jeremy's number plate (H982 FKL) has caused outrage and that the presenters should stay in the hotel room. Discussions between the producers and a representative of the protesters fail to ease the tension, who believe that Jeremy's registration plate was a deliberate reference to the Falklands War, and they are given just three hours to completely pack their kit and get out of Argentina. Despite complying, they are apparently intentionally slowed down by a truck ahead of them and then are attacked by a mob, who throw eggs, rocks and pick-axe handles at the crew, two of who gets hurt. They abandon the presenters' cars (as they are believed to be the cause of the incident) and leave across the road that they came (going across the lake without the pickup truck), retreating to Chile.

The morning light reveals the damage: many of the crews' cars had been hit, their windows and door mirrors broken. In the ending scene, Jeremy, Richard and James discuss what to do in a cabin, before jumping out in a Butch-Cassidy style ending sequence. During the end credits, each member of the cast and crew's first name was credited as "Robert Leroy", in homage to Robert Leroy Parker (better known as Butch Cassidy), American bank and train robber.

Lamborghini Huracán

Hammond reviews the new Lamborghini Huracán. While he is impressed with the car's acceleration, top speed, its gearbox and its handling, which are a real step up from the Gallardo and from Lambos of old, Hammond felt that to have fun with the Huracán you need your own test track as well as pointing out that though it is a somewhat beautiful car it doesn't have the presence that a Lamborghini should have, believing its makers had decided to play it "safe"; his point is proven by a montage consisting of all the previous Lambos reviewed by Hammond. Hammond concludes by saying that although the Huracán is a better car than previous Lambos, the previous cars are better Lambos due to them both looking and feeling more special, which Clarkson agrees. However, the Stig posts a lap time of 1.15.8, making the Huracán faster than the McLaren MP4-12C and faster than its big brother the Aventador; it also makes it the fastest Lamborghini to have gone around the Top Gear Test Track.

Australian Northern Territory Road Trip in GT's

Clarkson, May, and Hammond travel through Australia's Northern Territory on a four day road trip from Darwin to a 3.2 million acre (13,000 km2) cattle station with the aim of herding herd cattle using just three modern GT cars. Jeremy opted for the BMW M6 Gran Coupe whilst Richard went for the Bentley Continental GT V8S and James took the Nissan GT-R. Before they leave, Jeremy points outthat the letters on James' number plate could be a monarchical reference and therefore potentially offensive to Australian republicans (a joke picked up and carried by the others in reference to their troubles in Patagonia where it was perceived by locals that Clarkson's licence plate had a secondary meaning).

On the first day of the trip Clarkson and May had debated whose car was the fastest, and performed a drag race on an abandoned Second World War airfield to find out. Hammond also took part despite fears that his Bentley had less power and would lose badly due to it not having launch control like the other two. James stopped shortly after the start, pointing out that Jeremy had challenged him on being fastest "off the line" and that he had clearly beaten him "off the line". Clarkson disputed May's claim, but video revealed that the Nissan was indeed first to set off using launch control (by 16 m (52 ft)), followed by the Bentley, with the M6 starting last as it struggled for traction. A second full-on race was agreed upon, without launch control and to the finish. The M6 won this race, followed by the Bentley, with the GT-R coming in last. After the race, the trio drove to their "motel" and "fish restaurant" set up by the producers which was infact a campsite next to a swamp, where they would camp and catch their supper from crocodile-infested waters.

On the second day, concerned about animals jumping out into the road, the trio set about testing their brakes. Using an empty stretch of straight road, each presenter had to accelerate to 60 mph (97 km/h), and then brake when they reached a checkered flag marker. The Highway Code claims that braking distance at this speed will be 240 ft (73 m). The three men quickly make a mockery of this distance with the 2.5 long tons (2.5 t) Bentley stopping in less than half the distance. The M6 managed an even shorter distance than the Bentley, despite having steel, not ceramic brakes. The GT-R braked faster than the Bentley, but was not as quick as the BMW. Despite the BMW's win, Clarkson says the test was not about the win, but about disproving the Highway Code. The next test of their cars was at the Frances Creek open pit iron mine. Here, they would each take their cars up the service road that ran along the walls of the mine. A benchmark time of 1:17.8 was set by the Stig's Australian cousin in a HSV Maloo GTS ute. Clarkson went first, and set a time of 1:31.6 in his M6 after turning his traction control off, whilst Hammond went second and managed a much faster time of 1:18.6 in his Bentley. May - who was confident of his car, but not his own skills - pulled the British Stig out of the boot of his GT-R. Driving well past the finish line, ostensibly to turn around, James switched places with the Stig and passed off a time of 1:13.3 as his own, leaving Clarkson suspicious of how May had managed to achieve that result.

After a second night of camping, the trio had to drive through the heat on the third day to reach their destination, overtaking three road trains with relative ease. Reaching the entry to the cattle station just as night had fallen, they eventually reached the homestead. With no spare beds, they were forced to camp for a third night. In the morning, the three were sent out on their main challenge – to find and herd 4,000 cattle into a large pen using their cars. The trio were staggered by the fact that the station was the same size as the southeast of England. Having difficulty finding the cattle they were to herd, they became excited upon discovering four and began herding them. This effort proved fruitless and Hammond bogged the Bentley as the terrain became sandy. The four cattle ran off into the bush, making any further effort toward a roundup impossible. However, when the trio at last discovered the herd, the sheer volume of cattle overwhelmed them. They were then forced to bring in back-up – a duo of Robinson R22 helicopters, whose skilled pilots work the dangerous job of rounding up cattle. With the cars assisting the helicopters, they managed to herd the cattle into the pen, declaring their efforts "ambitious, but not rubbish".

Back in the studio, the presenters remarked with amazement that all three cars had travelled to the cattle station and done the final challenge without breaking down. However, when trying to choose the best car out of the three, both Hammond and May claimed theirs was the best, which soon led them to arguing about the flaws of each other's car (and Clarkson's as well). Clarkson, after he stopped them arguing, pointed out his BMW was the best, but stated he would not buy one, owing to the depreciation on the M6. However, when faced with choosing one of the other two cars, Clarkson revealed he'd rather ignore his car's flaws and still go for it.

Ambulance Challenge

Jeremy Clarkson, Richard Hammond and James May conduct a valuable piece of consumer research with their attempts to improve and enhance the ambulance.

Starting with a belief that current ambulances, which are usually very big and based on a diesel van, are in need of a rethink, the presenters go their separate ways to focus on the one area they think could be improved. May focuses on passenger comfort, Hammond tries to improve response times by getting other drivers out of the way more effectively, while Clarkson confronts the same issue with the invention of what he calls 'the sports ambulance'.

Their three very different creations are then put to the test with a series of severe and often messy challenges, culminating in a fast reaction to a spectacular emergency.

Jeremy and James attempt to rescue Richard in Canada

Richard Hammond is dropped into the remote, frozen wastes of Canada to test a watch with a built-in emergency beacon. Normally, activating the device would summon a vast international rescue crew, but in Hammond's case, the distress signal is sent directly to Jeremy Clarkson and James May who are disorganised, disinterested and very many miles away. Eventually, the pair get their hands on two machines they believe are suitable for the job and set off on an epic adventure to find their colleague.

The Track

The Top Gear test track and studios are located at Dunsfold Aerodrome in Surrey. The track itself is formed out of the runway and was designed by Lotus as a testing facility. Many former Lotus Formula 1 drivers have tested there over the years. Prior to its racing days, the Aerodrome had been built during the Second World War by the Royal Canadian Air Force who cleared the two hundred acres of woodland, which had previously laid the site, by planting plastic explosives under the trees and literally blowing them from the ground. This meant that the site was cleared and constructed in only six months. The first squadrons based at the aerodrome were 400, 414, and 430 Squadrons of the Royal Canadian Air Force equipped with Curtiss P-40 Tomahawks and North American P-51 Mustangs. They were followed by the North American B-25 Mitchell Mk II medium bombers of No. 139 Wing RAF, consisting of 98 and 180 Squadrons RAF, and 320 Squadron (formed from Dutch Naval Aviation Service personnel). When 139 Wing departed for the continent in the autumn of 1944, 83 Group Support Unit (later 83 Group Disbandment Centre) arrived with Spitfires, Typhoons and Tempests. After the war the airfield was used by the RAF to repatriate prisoners of war.

Dunsfold was declared inactive by the Royal Air Force in 1946 but was then used by Skyways Ltd, with York, Lancastrian, Skymaster, Rapide and Dove aircraft. Skyways' operations included support of the Berlin Airlift. Skyways also refurbished ex-RAF Spitfires and Hawker Hurricanes for the Portuguese Air Force.

In 1950 The Hawker Aircraft Company acquired the lease of the site. Dunsfold became internationally known for development of the Hunter jet fighter; limited numbers of Sea Hawks were also produced and Sea Furies were refurbished. Airwork Ltd leased two hangars from 1953-58 for the refurbishment of North American F-86 Sabres and Supermarine Attackers.

In October 1960 the then Hawker Siddeley flight tested its Hawker P.1127 prototype, the development aircraft that led to the Hawker Siddeley Harrier, the first VTOL jet fighter bomber. Folland Gnat test flying and production moved to Dunsfold from Chilbolton, Hampshire, in 1961. Final assembly of the Harrier and the Hawk trainer aircraft was also at Dunsfold.

Hawker Siddeley became part of British Aerospace in 1977. On 2 July 1986 British Aerospace's deputy chief test pilot Jim Hawkins was killed at Dunsfold when his developmental Hawk 200 crashed. On 24 June 1999 British Aerospace announced the closure of Dunsfold as part of a restructuring; Hawk final assembly had been transferred to Warton in 1988, the BAe Sea Harrier production finished in 1998 and the Harrier 2+ production was moved to Brough in 2000. The gate guardian aircraft - Hawker P.1127 XP984 - was moved to Brooklands Museum on long term loan.

Over the years, Dunsfold has seen many incidents and action. On 20 November 1975 a test flight of a Hawker Siddeley HS.125 G-BCUX was taking off on runway 07 when, just as aircraft became airborne, the flight was struck by birds. The pilots tried to land back onto the runway but the aircraft overran the runway and struck a passing car on the A281 road. The aircraft stopped in a field and was destroyed by fire. All six people inside the car died, and one crew member out of nine passengers and crew was injured.

On 2 July 1986 British Aerospace's deputy chief test pilot Jim Hawkins was killed at Dunsfold when his developmental Hawk 200 ZG200 crashed into farmland just beyond the road outside the airfield's southern boundary.

On 5 June 1998 a Hawker Hunter (G-HHUN) crashed at Dunsfold prior to that weekend's airshow. The pilot, John Davis, was killed.

When watching the many cars speeding around the Top Gear track, there can clearly be seen a white jumbo jet in the background. This is a Boeing 747-200 which served with British Airways until 2002 as City of Birmingham, G-BDXJ, and was purchased by Aces High Limited, a company specialising in supplying aircraft for television and film work, and transferred to Dunsfold. It was modified and used for filming for the 2006 James Bond film 'Casino Royale'. Programmes and commercials.

In 2009, for major parts of Episode 4 of ITV Series 'Primeval' featuring a giganotosaurus, Dunsfold was used as the location for an unspecified London airport.

In 2013, for the closing sequences of the film 'Red 2', Dunsfold was used as an undisclosed airfield near London. Both the Boeing 747-200 and the Dakota aircraft regularly visible in the background of Top Gear's test track features are seen during the closing car chase of the film.

The track's main route, marked by painted lines and simple structures such as stacks of tyres, was designed by test drivers from Lotus. The layout of the track is designed to put the car through various conditions, ranging from provoking understeer to testing brake balance and tyres. The track is approximately 1.75 miles (2.82 km) long. It is considered to be an equaliser for cars since, according to Richard Hammond, both 0–60 miles per hour (0–96.6 km/h) times and top speed are totally meaningless.]The track also incorporates a drag strip; although this is not used for timed segments, it does feature in some challenges and other features on the show.

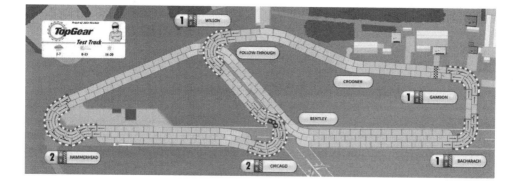

The course starts on the perimeter road outside the Top Gear studio. The first bend is a fast right-left kink named "Crooner Curves." "Wilson Bend" is the first proper turn on the track and the first corner usually seen when The Stig is lapping a car. "Chicago", a long right-hand around a tyre wall onto the main runway, was designed by Lotus as a steady state corner, designed to highlight understeer or oversteer of the chassis. Next is "Hammerhead", a left-then-right corner, which again highlights understeer and oversteer. The track comes to a right-hand curve, and then the course turns right through the flat-out section called the "Follow Through". After the left hand "Bentley Bend" named after the person who first "discovered" Jeremy Clarkson and former Top Gear presenter, Jon Bentley, but commonly referred to simply as "the tyres", the course comes to "Bacharach Bend", which, after the first series, has been referred to as the "Penultimate Corner" or the "Second-to-last Corner" and is often regarded as one of the most challenging on the course. The final turn before the finish line is "Gambon" in honour of Sir Michael Gambon, who completed the turn on two wheels in episode 8 of Series 1. Prior to this, the corner was known as "Carpenters Corner.

Power Laps

To be eligible to appear on the Power Lap Times board, a vehicle must be a road-legal production car and must have sufficient ride height to clear a standard speed bump, although occasionally vehicles that cannot appear on the list are still timed. Whenever a 'non-qualifying vehicle' is raced, the time is compared to the official Power Laps but then removed from the board. The Ferrari FXX owned by Michael Schumacher (1:10.7) was taken off the board after because it both failed to meet road legal standards and used slick tyres.

All laps are timed with the car's manufacturer-provided adjustable settings configured for maximum performance — all adjustable suspensions are set at their most efficient, all gear shift maps are at their most aggressive, and driving aids such as traction control are deactivated. Lap times do not offer complete comparisons between the cars, mainly because wet or otherwise poor weather conditions can negatively affect lap times.

Sometimes an additional term is written next to the time (such as Hot). This indicates that The Stig and the Top Gear team consider that the prevalent weather conditions have affected the lap time or car's performance. The time on the board is not changed: e.g. 1:50 MM (Mildly Moist) is deemed to be equivalent to 1:48 on a normal dry track. The following list describes how many seconds it costs a car or gives a car an advantage. These adjustments are not applicable to Formula 1 drivers.

- HOT = Track surface or car performance affected by high temperature or humidity (+1 second)
- Mildly moist (MM) / Damp (D) = Track surface slightly damp with some dry patches after light rain or drizzle   (+2 seconds)
- Moist (M) = Track surface slightly wet due to shower of rain (+3 seconds)
- Wet (W) / Melted snow (MS) = Track surface wet due to light rain or melted snow (+4 seconds)
- Very wet (VW) = Track surface wet (with large puddles) due to heavy rain −6 seconds
- Very very wet or flipping wet (FW) = Track surface wet (with flood water) due to heavy rain (8 seconds)
    - Snow (Snow) Track covered in snow (partially defrosted) (only used once; listed on its own board)

Suzuki Liana (2002–2005)

For the first seven series, the car driven for lap times was a Suzuki Liana. When first introduced, the car was worth just under £10,000. The car used is stock except for a roll cage and racing seats added as safety measures. Each guest practices with The Stig before making several attempts to complete the test track in the fastest time.

The two slowest laps on the Liana celebrity list are held by Terry Wogan and the late Richard Whiteley, both of whom were beaten by Billy Baxter, a Bosnian war veteran who is completely blind. He guided the Liana through the track under direction from Clarkson in the passenger seat in a time of 2 minutes 2 seconds, which was 1.4 seconds quicker than Terry Wogan, and 4 seconds faster than Richard Whiteley.

The fastest non-professional driver was Ellen MacArthur. Unlike most contenders she made no comments to the camera during her lap. She completed the lap in 1 minute 46.7 seconds, beating Jimmy Carr by 0.2 seconds.

The fastest lap ever completed by the Liana was by Lewis Hamilton, who drove round in 1.42.9, 1.5 seconds faster than The Stig.

The Liana endured considerable abuse from the stars while undertaking their laps. In one incident, actor Michael Gambon clipped the final corner, taking the car onto two wheels. It was done in such a spectacular fashion that the corner was named "Gambon Corner". When Lionel Richie drove the Liana, one of the front wheels fell off, invoking Clarkson to coin the term "pulling a Lionel". Trevor Eve also lost a wheel. The former British transport minister Stephen Ladyman added further injury to the Liana by denting the boot when he lost control during practice and slid backwards into a tyre wall. David Soul destroyed the gearbox of two Lianas during his time on the show due to his rough driving style. Patrick Kielty broke the Liana's front suspension during series 4 when he drove on the grass. Christopher Eccleston was the only celebrity to use a Liana with an automatic transmission, because a hesitant Eccleston admitted he was "only qualified to drive an automatic." To accommodate his needs, Top Gear succeeded in borrowing an automatic Liana, of which only 40 existed in the UK. As a reference to his role in Doctor Who, the automatic Liana was shown materialising onto the racing track, with a Tardis sound effect played over it.

The Liana has also been modified on several occasions. David Soul's Liana featured a red police light and a white stripe in reference to his Starsky and Hutch role. Johnny Vegas was provided with L-plates as he had not passed his driving test at the time. When Justin Hawkins came on the show, the Liana he drove had flame decals pasted on it. Actor Sanjeev Bhaskar had an ornate tissue box placed in the back, a homage to Indian drivers.

In its service, the Liana covered 1,600 laps of the circuit; went through 400 tyres; its brakes were changed 100 times; and it required six new clutches, two new hubs, driveshafts, wishbones, struts and gear linkages and a replacement wing mirror.

In July 2005, Formula One driver Damon Hill appeared on the show for the first time as the star. This was kept a surprise to the audience and the viewing public, and when Nigel Mansell came on the show, it was covered up in magazines and on the internet by saying that the Star in a Reasonably Priced Car would be Alan Titchmarsh.

For some of the laps more than one person has been present in the car. This was the case for Clarkson's run when he had both Hammond and Jason Dawe in the car. Trinny and Susannah were both in the car for each other's runs. Denise Van Outen was in Johnny Vaughan's when he did his lap; Van Outen never did a lap driving the car. Clarkson was also present as a navigator for Billy Baxter's laps.

Liana leaderboard

1. 1:46.7 – Ellen MacArthur
2. 1:46.9 – Jimmy Carr
3. 1:47.1 – Simon Cowell
4. 1:47.3 – Ronnie O'Sullivan
5. 1:47.8 – Ian Wright
6. 1:47.9 – Chris Evans
7. 1:47.9 – Rory Bremner
8. 1:48.0 – Trevor Eve
9. 1:48.0 – Justin Hawkins
10. 1:48.0 – Paul McKenna
11. 1:48.0 – Jodie Kidd
12. 1:48.0 – Jay Kay[28]
13. 1:48.0 – Patrick Kielty
14. 1:48.6 – Rob Brydon
15. 1:48.8 – Stephen Ladyman
16. 1:49.0 – Neil Morrissey
17. 1:49.7 – Roger Daltrey (mildly moist)
18. 1:50.0 – Martin Clunes
19. 1:50.0 – Jeremy Clarkson (with passengers)
20. 1:50.0 – Lionel Richie
21. 1:50.0 – Cliff Richard
22. 1:50.0 – Patrick Stewart
23. 1:50.0 – Jamie Oliver
24. 1:50.0 – Gordon Ramsay
25. 1:50.7 – David Walliams
26. 1:51.0 – Ranulph Fiennes
27. 1:51.1 – Timothy Spall
28. 1:51.2 – Carol Vorderman (mildly moist)
29. 1:51.3 – James Nesbitt
30. 1:51.4 – Christian Slater
31. 1:51.5 – Joanna Lumley
32. 1:51.5 – Omid Djalili
33. 1:51.5 – Sanjeev Bhaskar (wet)
34. 1:52.0 – David Dimbleby
35. 1:52.0 – Rick Parfitt
36. 1:52.0 – Eddie Izzard
37. 1:52.0 – Jordan
38. 1:52.4 – Christopher Eccleston (automatic)
39. 1:52.7 – Tim Rice
40. 1:53.0 – Vinnie Jones

41. 1:53.2 – Johnny Vaughan (with passenger Denise van Outen, originally 1:53.4)
42. 1:53.3 – Fay Ripley (midly moist)
43. 1:53.4 – Bill Bailey (wet)
44. 1:53.5 – Jack Dee
45. 1:54.0 – Steve Coogan (wet, originally stated to be 1:53)
46. 1:54.0 – Ross Kemp (wet)
47. 1:54.0 – Alan Davies (wet)
48. 1:54.0 – Stephen Fry (moist)
49. 1:54.0 – Tara Palmer-Tomkinson
50. 1:54.0 – David Soul
51. 1:54.0 – Rich Hall
52. 1:54.0 – Martin Kemp (wet)
53. 1:54.1 – Trinny Woodall (very wet, with passenger Susannah Constantine)
54. 1:55.0 – Michael Gambon (wet)
55. 1:55.4 – Geri Halliwell
56. 1:55.7 – Susannah Constantine (very wet, with passenger Trinny Woodall)
57. 1:56.0 – Boris Johnson
58. 1:57.0 – Anne Robinson
59. 1:57.0 – Jonathan Ross (penalised for cutting a corner)
60. 1:57.1 – Davina McCall (very wet)
61. 1:58.6 – Johnny Vegas (provisionally licensed)
62. 2:01.0 – Harry Enfield
63. 2:02.0 – Billy Baxter (blind man with Clarkson as passenger guide)
64. 2:03.4 – Terry Wogan (originally listed as 2:04)
65. 2:06.0 – Richard Whiteley

Chevrolet Lacetti (2006–2009)

Starting with the eighth series, the Liana was replaced by a Chevrolet Lacetti and a new blank scoreboard. The format was changed so that each star would have five practice laps, and then a final timed lap, with no allowance being given for mishaps.

As a starter for the new car and format, an open day was held for any celebrity who wanted to take part. Seven stars recorded times that day:

James Hewitt (who Jeremy and Richard referred to as the 'Well Spoken Man' after failing to recognise him), comedians Alan Davies and Jimmy

Carr, rock stars Rick Wakeman and Justin Hawkins, footballer Les Ferdinand, and actor Trevor Eve who topped the time at 1 minute 47.0 seconds. Jimmy Carr, who held second place in the Liana behind Ellen MacArthur, spun off while doing his timed lap and got the second to one slowest time ever around the track at 2 minutes, 8.91 seconds.

On 28 January 2007, Jamie Oliver posted a time of 1:47.70 in melted snow and standing water. Given the rivalry Oliver felt towards fellow celebrity chef, and then-lapboard leader, Gordon Ramsay, Oliver asked that the 4-second allowance normally granted for wet laps be used to put him at the top of the leaderboard "just for a day".

Actress Billie Piper posted a time of 1:48.3 but was deemed by The Stig to have failed to complete a lap properly, as she failed to negotiate some corners. The Stig suggested a three-second time penalty, but after Clarkson consulted the audience, it was decided to let the time stand, which her Doctor Who co-star, David Tennant, tried to overturn on 23 December 2007 show, at the end of the following series. Clarkson remarked that if Tennant had worn a see through top (like Piper for her interview), he "would have been faster than Simon Cowell".

In 11 November 2007 episode, Simon Cowell retook his status as the holder of the fastest lap with a time of 1:45.90. According to Clarkson, the cameramen said they had never seen such consistency in the practice laps. However, Cowell was knocked off the top spot in Series 11 by Jay Kay, who now holds the fastest time in the Lacetti, although Clarkson selected the fastest of Jay Kay's times rather than the last run, which was slower than Cowell's time, seemingly due to a dislike of Cowell (he claimed earlier in the episode that Cowell had been at the top of the leaderboard for too long). Had this not happened, Cowell would have been knocked off the top by Grand Designs host Kevin McCloud.

Clarkson has referred to the part of the board with times of 1:51 and over as the 'Thespian Zone' due to the propensity for classically trained actors to post slow times.

Series 11 featured a slight change to the format, with two 'Stars' per episode instead of the previous one (although there had been a couple of editions in previous series' with more than one guest). Each of the pair are professionally associated with their fellow guest, usually both either act in or present the same TV show. Unlike previous episodes where two stars have appeared, the stars drove individual laps without the other present in the car.

On 28 March 2010, Richard Hammond attended the demolition of the two 550 ft chimneys at Lafarge Cement's Northfleet Works. On the first episode of Series 15, it was shown that the Lacetti was partially crushed by placing it in the path of one of the falling chimneys.

Lacetti leaderboard

1.   1:45.81 – Jay Kay
2.   1:45.85 – Brian Johnson
3.   1:45.87 – Kevin McCloud
4.   1:45.9 – Simon Cowell
5.   1:46.1 – Jennifer Saunders
6.   1:46.3 – Michael Sheen
7.   1:46.3 – Gordon Ramsay
8.   1:46.5 – Usain Bolt
9.   1:46.9 – Peter Jones
10.   1:47.0 – Trevor Eve
11.   1:47.1 – Peter Firth
12.   1:47.4 – Lawrence Dallaglio
13.   1:47.4 – Les Ferdinand

14.   1:47.5 – Eric Bana (wet)
15.   1:47.6 – James Hewitt
16.   1:47.7 – Jamie Oliver (melted snow and standing water)
17.   1:47.7 – Hugh Grant
18.   1:48.0 – Ewan McGregor
19.   1:48.1 – Rupert Penry-Jones
20.   1:48.1 – Chris Evans (wet)
21.   1:48.3 – James Blunt (wet)
22.   1:48.3 – Billie Piper (cut corner, penalty not added)
23.   1:48.4 – Justin Hawkins
24.   1:48.5 – Simon Pegg
25.   1:48.5 – Theo Paphitis (written as Theo Pamphlet)
26.   1:48.7 – Mark Wahlberg
27.   1:48.7 – Michael McIntyre
28.   1:48.8 – David Tennant
29.   1:48.8 – Jay Leno
30.   1:48.9 – Will Young (damp)
31.   1:49.4 – Michael Parkinson
32.   1:49.6 – Ronnie Wood
33.   1:49.7 – Harry Enfield
34.   1:49.8 – Sienna Miller
35.   1:49.9 – Jools Holland
36.   1:50.3 – Michael Gambon
37.   1:50.3 – Alan Davies
38.   1:50.9 – Steve Coogan (hot)
39.   1:51.0 – Stephen Fry (hot)
40.   1:51.2 – Alan Carr
41.   1:51.4 – Ray Winstone (hot)
42.   1:51.7 – Keith Allen (very wet)
43.   1:51.7 – Rob Brydon (wet)
44.   1.51.8 – Seasick Steve (moist)
45.   1:51.8 – Justin Lee Collins
46.   1:52.2 – Tom Jones
47.   1:52.5 – Guy Ritchie (wet)
48.   1:52.8 – Dame Helen Mirren
49.   1:53.4 – James Corden (wet)
50.   1:54.0 – Kristin Scott Thomas
51.   1:54.3 – Philip Glenister (wet)
52.   1:54.7 – Kate Silverton (very wet)
53.   1:55.3 – Rick Wakeman
54.   1:57.4 – Boris Johnson (very wet)
55.   1:57.4 – Fiona Bruce (very wet)
56.   2:01:0 – Brian Cox

57.   2:08.9 – Jimmy Carr (spun off on timed lap)

Kia Cee'd (2010–2013)

In the last episode of the fourteenth series of the show, Clarkson revealed that they were thinking about getting a new Reasonably Priced Car for the next series. On 27 June, during the first episode of the fifteenth series, it was revealed to be the Kia Cee'd (refered to by Clarkson as the "Cee-apostrophe-d) and, as with the Chevrolet Lacetti, another open day was held to welcome the new car. Nick Robinson, Peter Jones, Al Murray, Bill Bailey, Peta Todd, Louie Spence and Amy Williams were among the initial drivers.

Cee'd leaderboard

1.   1:42.1 – Matt LeBlanc
2.   1:42.2 – Rowan Atkinson
3.   1:42.8 – Michael Fassbender (ice on the second-to-last corner)
4.   1:42.8 – John Bishop
5.   1:43.5 – Ross Noble
6.   1:43.6 – James McAvoy
7.   1:43.7 – Ryan Reynolds
8.   1:43.7 – Matt Smith
9.   1:44.2 – Tom Cruise
10.   1:44.4 – Amy Macdonald
11.   1:44.5 – Nick Frost
12.   1:44.9 – Simon Pegg
13.   1:45.2 – Cameron Diaz
14.   1:45.2 – Alex James
15.   1:45.4 – Mick Fleetwood
16.   1:45.5 – Rupert Grint
17.   1:45.9 – Peter Jones
18.   1:45.9 – Boris Becker (wet)
19.   1:46.1 – Andy García

20.   1.46.8 – Bill Turnbull
21.   1:47.0 – Alastair Campbell
22.   1:47.7 – Louis Walsh
23.   1:47.8 – Sophie Raworth
24.   1:47.8 – Danny Boyle (wet)
25.   1:48.1 – Al Murray
26.   1:48.1 – Bob Geldof
27.   1:49.0 – Jeff Goldblum
28.   1:49.0 – Jonathan Ross (wet)
29.   1:49.4 – will.i.am (wet) (automatic)
30.   1:49.8 – Slash (wet)
31.   1:49.9 – Nick Robinson
32.   1:49.9 – Peta Todd (damp)
33.   1:50.3 – Amber Heard (automatic)
34.   1:50.5 – Fiona Bruce
35.   1:50.8 – Bill Bailey (wet)
36.   1:50.9 – Amy Williams (wet)
37.   1:53.3 – Johnny Vaughan (wet)
38.   1:53.69 – Louie Spence (wet)
39.   1:56.3 – Alice Cooper (wet + automatic)
40.   1.56.7 – John Prescott (wet + automatic)
41.   2:09.1 – Damian Lewis (snow)

Vauxhall Astra (2013–2015)

In the first episode of series 20, Clarkson and Hammond revealed their new Reasonably Priced Car – A 1.6 'Tech Line' Vauxhall Astra. In similar fashion to earlier "new starts", an open day was held for multiple stars to drive the car.

Astra leaderboard

1. 1:44.2 - Olly Murs
2. 1:44.7 - Nicholas Hoult
3. 1:44.7 – Aaron Paul
4. 1:45.1 – Brian Johnson
5. 1:45.6 – Jimmy Carr
6. 1:45.1 – Hugh Jackman
7. 1:46.7 – David Haye
8. 1:46.8 – Warwick Davis
9. 1:47.1 – Margot Robbie
10. 1:47.2 – Will Smith
11. 1:47.8 – Benedict Cumberbatch
12. 1:48.5 – Rachel Riley
13. 1:48.5 – Gillian Anderson (Very Wet)
14. 1:48.8 – Charles Dance
15. 1:48.9 – Joss Stone
16. 1:49.2 – Kiefer Sutherland
17. 1:49.4 – James Blunt (very very wet)
18. 1:49.9 – Ron Howard
19. 1:49.9 – Tom Hiddleston (very wet)
20. 1:50.1 – Hugh Bonneville (wet)
21. 1:51.0 – Steven Tyler
22. 1:51.5 – Mike Rutherford
23. 1:54.3 – Ed Sheeran
24. 1.54.5 – Jack Whitehall (automatic)

F1 drivers

All Formula One drivers are put into their own list with regard to lap times because of their exceptional skill level. When the Liana was pulled out from retirement to allow Jenson Button to make a time, Clarkson noted that the Liana would be pulled out for use by Formula 1 drivers in the future.

The original 'black' Stig and the first 'white' Stig have done laps around the track in the Suzuki Liana. Both had their times removed from the leaderboard upon their departure.

On 6 July 2011, Sebastian Vettel managed to top the board with a time of 1:44.0. Vettel's lap was the first time someone taking a 'Formula One drivers' line through the first corner was able to top The Stig's time, as Rubens Barrichello took the tighter line. Jeremy also mentioned on this episode that the current Stig has yet to do a lap of the track in the Liana, therefore there is currently no time on the board for the Stig.

On 17 February 2013, Lewis Hamilton returned to do a dry lap and lowered the F1 Drivers record by 1.1s to 1:42.9. This was in the wake of his move to Mercedes AMG for the 2013 season. Lewis beat his old McLaren teammate Jenson Button by 1.8 seconds.

1 Daniel Ricciardo   1:42.2
2 Lewis Hamilton   1:42.9 Second attempt
3 Mark Webber   1:43.1 Second attempt
4 Sebastian Vettel   1:44.0
5 Rubens Barrichello   1:44.3
6 Ben Collins   1:44.4 The Stig II (Removed from the board during interview with Vettel).
7 Nigel Mansell   1:44.6
8 Lewis Hamilton   1:44.7 Wet & oily
9 Jenson Button   1:44.7 Hot
10 Jenson Button   1:44.9 Second attempt. Wet
11 Perry McCarthy   1:46.0 The Stig I (Removed from the board).
12 Kimi Räikkönen   1:46.1 Very wet
13 Damon Hill   1:46.3
14 Mark Webber   1:47.1 Extremely wet

SPIN OFFS

Top Gear Australia

Top Gear Australia premiered on the 'SBS One' channel on the 29th September 2008 at 7:30 pm (Australian time) with its first season consisting of 8 episodes. A second season was announced following the release of ratings figures for the premiere and favourable comments from advertisers, and began airing from 11 May 2009. After acquiring the rights to broadcast the UK version in 2009, the 'Nine Network' started airing their own version of Top Gear Australia in September 2010. Top Gear Australia returned for a fourth season in 2011. The show has since been cancelled as of 14 September 2011 due to declining ratings.

Prior to filming SBS made an open casting call for presenters, resulting in over 4000 applications. The original hosts chosen for Top Gear Australia were cartoonist and motoring columnist Warren Brown, MotoGP commentator Charlie Cox, and race driver / driving instructor Steve Pizzati.

Marketing prior to the first episode stated that the presenters would be joined by The Stig's "Australian cousin", but in the first episode the driver was introduced as just "The Stig". Steve Pizzati suggested that The Stig have an "Australian" name, such as "Stiggo", but the other presenters refused. The season 2 opener clarified that Top Gear Australia's Stig is not intended to be the same Stig from the UK series.

On 19 December 2008, Charlie Cox announced he was leaving the program as he felt he was unable to offer enough time to the show. SBS subsequently announced that a Trumpeter (no wonder it was cancelled) called James Morrison would be his replacement, joining Warren and Steve for season two. Morrison had previously appeared as a guest in the sixth episode.

For the third season, early reports claimed that former Australian cricketer Shane Warne would take over the hosting of the show alongside Jeremy Clarkson, although the BBC ultimately ruled out Clarkson's involvement in the Australian version. On 20 June 2010, it was announced that actor and comedian Shane Jacobson and Top Gear Australia magazine editor Ewen Page would join a returning Steve Pizzati to present the show for the Nine Network, which premièred on 28 September 2010 with a 75-minute The Ashes special, in which the hosts faced off against their Top Gear UK counterparts in a series of motoring-related challenges. The UK presenters won after cheating in the final challenge by using a professional race driver instead of James May.

Mirroring the UK series, the studio segments were recorded at Bankstown Airport in Sydney. An exact copy of the UK studio at Dunsfold Park was constructed in a hangar (Hangar Building 581). The power laps and "Star in a Bog Standard Car" were recorded at Camden Airport with parts of the runways and taxiways used as a test track.

Top Gear Russia

Top Gear Russia (Russian: Top Gear: Русская версия) was a Russian motoring television series on 'Ren-TV'. 'It premiered on 22 February 2009.

The hosts chosen for Top Gear Russia were Nikolai Fomenko, former musician (as part of Secret band, former race car driver, theater actor and TV presenter. He is also involved in the creation of the Russian supercar Marussia. Mikhail Petrovsky, actor, automotive journalist and blogger, & Oskar Kuchera, ex-MTV Russia presenter and actor.

Similar to both the original UK series and its Australian spin-off, Top Gear Russia features a Power lap segment, in this case held in an abandoned airfield in Mnevniki. To inaugurate the track and populate the lap board in the first episode, the hosts invited numerous local celebrities to participate and treated them to a picnic with shashlyk and a smoking samovar.

The 'Reasonably-Priced Car' is a race-prepped Lada Kalina.

Top Gear US

In 2005, the 'Discovery Channel' made a pilot for an American version of the show featuring actor and IHRA driver Bruno Massel as one of the hosts, but it was not picked up by the network. A short time later Discovery Channel began airing a slightly "Americanized" version of the British Top Gear show with presenters Jeremy Clarkson, Richard Hammond, and James May. This show featured clips of features and challenges from Series 1–5 from the BBC Two show with introduction segments recorded by Clarkson, Hammond and May at the Dunsfold Aerodrome studio especially for the US audience. Regular features like "The News" and "Star in a Reasonably Priced Car" were not shown on the Discovery Channel version.

In April 2007, the BBC were still looking to export an American produced version of Top Gear to the United States. NBC announced, in January 2008, that it had ordered a pilot for an American version of the show, retitled Gear. BBC Worldwide had been contracted to produce the pilot for NBC. According to NBC reality chief Craig Plestis, many automakers had shown interest in America's version of Top Gear.

On June 16, 2008, NBC and the BBC officially announced an American version of Top Gear, to be hosted by Adam Carolla, Tanner Foust and Eric Stromer. The studio segments for the pilot were taped on July 26, 2008 to generally favorable reviews citing close following of the UK version's format. NBC was expected to have Top Gear premiere as a midseason replacement in 2009.

Jay Leno, who originally turned down offers to host the show, expressed concern in 2008 over whether or not a show like Top Gear could be successful in America. In a column published by The Sunday Times in 2008, Leno expressed concern that an American version could lack the critical reviews for which the British version is known. The British show is produced for the BBC with public funds while the American show airs on commercial television. Leno believes that the show may have to worry about offending current and potential sponsors by giving their products poor reviews, leading to a compromise in the journalistic integrity and freedom of the original show.

On December 11, 2008, NBC reversed its decision to place the show as a midseason replacement, citing concerns about the potential success of a car-themed show in light of the failure of Knight Rider. NBC allowed the BBC to shop it around to cable networks to possibly pick it up. In February 2009, Jeremy Clarkson stated that the American version had been "canned", claiming that focus groups "... just don't understand a single word we're on about. They just don't get it really."

On August 6, 2010, the first Top Gear trailer was published on the web, giving fans a preview on what to expect on the upcoming episodes to be broadcast on the History Channel. In this trailer, new hosts Adam Ferrara, Tanner Foust, and Rutledge Wood were seen participating in a Moonshine Challenge and Tanner Foust also takes a Dodge Viper for a test drive. The first season premiered on November 21, 2010, and the series has been renewed for a second season. Commenting on the recently announced second season renewal, UK host Jeremy Clarkson noted, "Top Gear is our baby so you can understand why Hammond, May and I were anxious about passing it on to the presenters of the US show. We needn't have worried because Top Gear is clearly in safe hands, even if they do insist on speaking in those stupid accents. Watching an episode from series 1 with Richard and James, we found ourselves in a genuinely heated debate about which of the presenters' cars was best. We were just three ordinary chaps watching a car show and loving it, which is exactly what Top Gear should be. Bring on series 2."

The show follows a similar format of the BBC version: three main hosts present, The Stig tests vehicles, and celebrities are invited for interviews and to drive vehicles around a test track. In addition, challenges similar in nature to the ones presented in the original show are replicated in Top Gear. The "Star in a Reasonably Priced Car" (retitled "Big Star, Small Car") segment uses a Suzuki SX4 Sportback. Filming of this segment, along with in-studio segments take place at the former Marine Corps Air Station El Toro, now known as the Orange County Great Park, in Irvine, California.

Producers of the History channels version have noted a greater interest in car customization by American car enthusiasts than in Britain. As of season 3, this element has been incorporated as the main focus of the show and the hosts no longer interview guests, review cars or produce Power Laps.

Top Gear South Korea

Top Gear Korea was announced on June 21, 2011, the show follows a similar format with the British version and season 1 included 3 presenters: singer and professional driver Kim Jin-pyo, actor Yeon Jung-hoon , and actor Kim Kap-soo. It premiered on cable channel XTM on August 20, 2011.

The show uses a circuit in Ansan city, which is not used for racing but just for tests and social events, as the main test facility and the Power Lap Time track. Korea International Circuit, the venue of Korean Grand Prix and Taebaek Racing Park are used for some episodes.

The first season aired from August 20 to December 30, 2011, met with both positive and negative reviews, the show had a peak viewership rating of 1.28%, considered to be quite good for Korean cable.

The second season aired from April 8, 2012 to June 17, 2012. Kim Kap-soo was replaced by actor Jo Min-ki

The third season (titled Top Gear Korea New Season) aired from October 7 to December 16, 2012. Jo Min-ki was replaced by actor Park Jun-gyu. In one of the episodes, presenter Kim Jin-pyo drove a Chevrolet Spark through a 360-degree vertical loop.

A serious incident occurred during filming of the fourth season, in which a helicopter crashed into the Arizona desert. As part of a racing sequence between a Chevrolet Corvette C6 ZR1 and a Bell AH-1 Cobra helicopter, the car and the helicopter would race alongside each other to the finish line. During a practice run, as they reached the finish line, the aircraft wheeled around 180° before impacting the ground. Nobody was seriously injured. The BBC, which owns the franchise, posted the video online, both in its unaltered state and open-captioned in English.

Guests are featured each week in the Star Lap Time segment, akin to Star in a Reasonably Priced Car. The car driven in this segment is the Volkswagen Golf.

Top Gear China

In May of 2014, the BBC announced that it has signed a deal with Honyee Media to produce a local version of Top Gear in China. On the 13th of November, 2014, the first series of the Top Gear China premiered on Shanghai Dragon Television, presented by Cheng Lei, a veteran Chinese TV presenter, Richie Jen, a Taiwanese singer and actor, and Tian Liang, a former Olympic gold-medalist in diving.

Top Gear France

A French version of Top Gear commenced filming at the end of 2014 at the aérodrome de Brienne-le-Château near Troyes. The first series began in early 2015 on the RMC Découverte free-to-air channel. It is presented by the actor Philippe Lellouche, the professional driver Bruce Jouanny and Yann Larret-Menezo, an electronic music artist and journalist.

The first episode, broadcast on the 18th of March 2015 at 20:45, broke RMC Découverte's audience record with 966,000 spectators (3.6% audience share)

Top Gear Rally Report

Rally Report was a series of program's broadcast by the BBC covering the Lombard RAC Rally of Great Britain - then the last round of the World Rally Championship.

It was transmitted on BBC2 during the 1980s and 1990s and usually featured previews, a live stage, twice nightly reports and a wrap-up compilation. The show was made at BBC Pebble Mill and later branded as Top Gear Rally Report since unusually it was not made by BBC Sport. Top Gear presenter William Woollard presented the programme from rally headquarters with Sue Baker, Barrie Gill and later Tony Mason doing the location reports on the stages.

In 1987 Tony Mason joined Top Gear - first as a rally specialist and then as a major contributor.

The show's theme music was "Jeweled" (from the remix album Wishful Thinking) by Propaganda

Top Gear Motorsport

Top Gear Motorsport covered various forms of motor racing. Broadcast on BBC Two from 1994 to 1998, the programme was presented by former Formula One driver and Top Gear presenter Tiff Needell. Other presenters were Penny Mallory, Tony Mason, Steve Berry, Mark James and Bob Constanduros.

The series covered a wide variety of motor racing categories, including the World Rally Championship, the British Rally Championship, British Formula Three, Formula Renault, and Formula Vauxhall Junior, British Superbikes, and Eurocars.

Stars in Fast Cars

Stars in Fast Cars was a
humorous motoring-themed
celebrity game show, in which
celebrities competed at
motoring challenges, including
recreating movie stunts and
racing modified armchairs. The
series was first broadcast on BBC Three, in 2005, and repeated on BBC
One in 2006.

Among some of the more notable moments were Car Skittles; a stunt where
the guests had to drive on to the back of a moving lorry, before letting them
all drive a Ferrari – with a bathtub of water attached to the back which they
were not allowed to spill. They were asked to race in a variety of "motor-
esque" machines, from the aforementioned armchairs to Formula 1 cars.
The final round of each show, between the two top-ranking guests, features
the use of the car cannon in attempts to hit various things.

Top Gear of the Pops

Top Gear of the Pops was a one-off special of Top Gear, broadcast in the
evening on 16 March 2007. It was shown as part of the Comic Relief 2007
appeal, mixing the usual elements of Top Gear with Top of the Pops, the
music chart show that was cancelled in 2006. The standard Top Gear
opening sequence had its car footage replaced with vintage clips of Top of

the Pops, and, while The Cool Wall
was mentioned at the beginning, it
was not included in the broadcast.
The programme was produced for
Comic Relief as a replacement for a
quiz show, A Question of Comedy,
which had been recorded some
months earlier but withdrawn
because the involvement of Jade
Goody as a contestant was felt
inappropriate following the
controversy surrounding her appearance on Celebrity Big Brother 5.

Top Ground Gear Force

This was a one-off TV special, featuring the cast of Top Gear, which originally aired on BBC Two at 22:00 GMT on 14 March 2008 as part of Sport Relief 2008.

It borrowed its format from Top Gear of the Pops. Whereas Top Gear of The Pops combined Top Gear with Top of the Pops, this episode combines the motoring show with Ground Force, a gardening makeover show which ran on the BBC from 1998 to 2005.

Jeremy Clarkson, James May and Richard Hammond take over sportsman Steve Redgrave's garden, to dispense advice on creating a zero maintenance lawn, installing an impressive water feature and getting rid of unwanted plants. Naturally, disaster ensues.

Like Top Gear of the Pops, the title screen and music is changed to suit the programme. Instead of having cars in the background, images of gardening were shown instead. The images bore a strong resemblance to the Top Gear title screen (e.g. dirt coming out of a spinning pot, similar to a car wheel spinning and kicking up water from the ground) Hammond was seen pushing a spade into the ground, and then holding it over his shoulder. May was seen holding a wheelbarrow, and breaking a gnome in half (in replacement of him pushing a button on a remote control in the Top Gear title screen). Clarkson was seen with a pair of open hedge trimmers, which he then snaps shut.

The Top Gear ending credits are also adapted to suit the program's resemblance to Ground Force – the presenters' names were listed as Alan Clarkson, Handy Hammond and Charlie May (references to Ground Force presenters Alan Titchmarsh, Tommy Walsh and Charlie Dimmock respectively).

The title Top Ground Gear Force appears during the opening credits and is spoken by the hosts throughout the show. However, the insulated jackets worn by the three hosts are silkscreened with "TGGGF" on the front chest and "Top Garden Ground Gear Force" on the rear. Other equipment, such as a flatbed truck, is labeled with the factual title, "Top Ground Gear Force". This minor detail is not explained throughout The Top Gear team of Jeremy Clarkson, James May and Richard Hammond decided, for Sport Relief, to resurrect the show Ground Force, and provide a garden makeover to the garden of one of Britain's

sporting legends, namely Sir Stephen Redgrave. Helping them was a team of Poles, and on hand to provide advice on Sir Steve's tastes was Ann Redgrave, who was erroneously addressed and referred to as "Lady Ann" rather than the proper "Lady Redgrave".

As the team's only 'country bumpkin', Hammond decided to designate himself as the team leader. However, his plan to build a 'river of gravel' failed to impress Clarkson and May, who wanted to include a water feature and a shed, respectively. Clarkson also noted that Hammond's river of gravel would pass through one of Redgrave's flowerbeds, which would be particularly difficult to remove. Hammond demonstrates that it is easy to simply dig up each flower with a trowel, Clarkson declares it would take too long, and instead reveals his unique method for removing the flowers using a shotgun. Unimpressed, Hammond sends Clarkson and May to Wyevale Garden Centre to pick up supplies. Deciding to go ahead with his plans to create a 'river of gravel', Hammond uses a small JCB digger to dig a trench in the garden. Meanwhile, Clarkson and May arrive back with their desired equipment, only to destroy the push bike of one of Redgrave's children as they pull into his drive. As May starts work on his shed, Clarkson enlists the help of the Poles to start work on his greenhouse. Meanwhile, unable to control his JCB, Hammond crashes it into the trench, leaving it immobile. In an attempt to rectify the situation, he hires a much larger JCB to pull the smaller one out of the hole, but due to the JCB being extremely heavy, it results in him leaving numerous caterpillar track marks all over the remainder of the garden lawn. Meanwhile, May has just completed work on his shed.

Hammond decides to leave both JCBs, and instead moves on to his next project - building a round-the-tree seat to be placed at the end of his 'river of gravel'. However, Clarkson quickly points out that despite the seat being complete, Hammond has no way of placing it around the tree, as it has been constructed as a sole piece. Clarkson offers to help Hammond by attempting to prune the tree with his shotgun, allowing the seat to be lifted and then dropped from the top of the tree. However, his gun misfires, and instead blasts a massive hole through the side of May's shed. Meanwhile, Hammond hires a 14-ton crane to lift his seat high enough to slip it over the tree. However, the crane is too heavy, and instead sinks into the lawn, leaving massive holes in it. However, he finds that the crane itself is long enough to still do the job, but his in experience means that instead of lifting the seat, he moves it sideways, crashing it into and destroying May's shed. May is extremely angry, but Clarkson appears amused by the situation.

May starts upon rebuilding the shed, and with the help of the Poles, the shed is quickly reinstated. He begins by labelling where each of the tools in the shed should go, alphabetically ordering the books on the bookshelf, and placing up pictures that he believes will remind Redgrave of his glory days.

Meanwhile, Clarkson has the tricky job of removing a rockery in order to build his water feature. He decides to use a homemade bomb to completely the job quickly. The bomb is successful, destroying the rockery in one clean sweep - but the blast is so powerful that the energy manages to blow all of the windows and one of the walls out of May's rebuilt shed, leaving him angrier than ever. May subsequently emerges from the shed, and asks Clarkson what time the programme will air. After being informed it was going to air after the watershed, he exclaims at Clarkson, 'you're a fu-'. At this point, the episode cuts to the next scene.

With Hammond at a loose end after the failure of both his 'river of gravel' and his tree seat, he begins to wander aimlessly. Meanwhile, Clarkson has ordered some cement to pave over the parts of the lawn which were destroyed by Hammond's giant digger and 14-ton crane. However, despite his estimations, he orders too little, and only a small portion of the lawn is covered. At this point, The Salvation Army brass band arrive to provide entertainment for the team, but their appearance is cut short when Hammond gets stuck in Clarkson's undried cement, and their musical accompaniment drives Clarkson insane, leading him to bend one of their trombones in half and ask them to leave. With Hammond having ruined Clarkson's cement by leaving footprints in it, Clarkson moves on to his next project - erecting some rugby posts, despite being told that none of Redgrave's family plays rugby. With May having successfully rebuilt his shed again, it's not long before disaster strikes again, when Clarkson and the Poles drop the rugby posts, and they fall directly on May's shed, destroying part of the roof and one of the side walls. By this point, May is fuming, and he screams at Clarkson to apologise, while pointing a two-by-four at him. After being successfully rescued from the cement, Hammond has moved on to his last project, a turbo-charged barbecue system, which allows the user to cook varieties of meat in under five minutes, using a jet engine to rotate the meat and cook it. Clarkson and May are impressed, until the blades begin to rotate too fast, and the chicken is flung off the rotisserie. May and Clarkson are amused by the situation, as all of Hammond's projects so far - the tree seat, river of gravel and barbecue - have all failed, while both May's shed, after being resurrected three times, and Clarkson's greenhouse, have both been successful. However, May's amusement is short-lived when the fire from the barbecue burns out of control, and manages to set fire to his once again newly rebuilt shed. Fuming, he attempts to put the fire out before it can take hold, but Clarkson takes hold of the fire extinguisher, forcing May to watch his shed burn. However, the team soon receive word that Redgrave is now pulling into the drive. Despite two abandoned JCBs, an abandoned crane, a burning shed, a ruined lawn and a destructive barbecue, the team are forced to go ahead and unveil the garden to Redgrave. At first, Redgrave is upset at the destruction of his garden, and storms inside his house, leaving the Poles to run away, with Clarkson proclaiming they can 'sense the mood'. Clarkson and May initially attempt to blame the entire debacle on Hammond, but eventually, after Clarkson talking to him privately, Redgrave's mood lightens. Despite all of Hammond and May's projects being failures, Clarkson manages to unveil his proudly built greenhouse, and his turbo-charged water feature. Redgrave is slightly impressed, until Clarkson activates the water feature. The gush of water is so powerful that it manages to burst the top off the water feature, sending gallons of water flying up into the air, and the broken half of the water feature crashing down through the greenhouse, smashing all of the windows and destroying some of the wooden structure.

Cars of the Year

At the end of each autumn series the hosts present an award to their favourite car of the year. The only criterion for the award is that all three presenters must come to a unanimous choice. Winners of the past years are:

2002   Land Rover Range Rover
2003   Rolls-Royce Phantom
2004   Volkswagen Golf GTI
2005   Bugatti Veyron
2006   Lamborghini Gallardo Spyder
2007   Subaru Legacy Outback/Ford Mondeo
2008   Caterham Seven R500
2009   Lamborghini Gallardo LP550-2 Valentino Balboni
2010   Citroën DS3
2011   Range Rover Evoque
2012   Toyota GT86
2013   Ford Fiesta ST
2014   James drove the Laferrari and choose the Laferrari
         Richard drove the 918 and choose the 918
         Jeremy drove the P1 and choose the Corvette

Power Lap Car used	Time (mins)
Ariel Atom V8	1.15.1
McLarenMP4-12C	1.16.2
Lamborghini Aventador	1.16.5
Bugatti Veyron SS	1.16.8
Gumpert Apollo	1.17.1
Ascari A10	1.17.3
Koenigsegg CCX (with Top Gear spoiler)	1.17.6
Noble M600	1.17.7
Pagani Zonda F Roadster	1.17.7
Caterham R500	1.17.9
Bugatti Veyron	1.18.3
Pagani Zonda F	1.18.4
Maserati MC12	1.18.9
Ferrari Enzo	1.19.0
Lamborghini LP670 SV	1.19.0
Ferrari 458	1.19.1
Ariel Atom	1.19.5
Lamborghini LP560	1.19.5
Ferrari Scuderia	1.19.7
Nissan GT-R	1.19.7
Ferrari GTO	1.19.8
Lamborghini LP640	1.19.8
Porsche Carerra GT	1.19.8
Koenigsegg CCX	1.20.4
Corvette ZR1	1.20.4
Ascari KZ1	1.20.7
Mercedes McLaren SLR	1.20.9

Power Lap Car used	Time (mins)
Ferrari 599GTB	1.21.2
Audi R8 V10	1.21.6
Ford GT	1.21.9
Porsche 911 Turbo Convertible	1.22.2
Audi R8 V10 Spyder	1.22.3
Ferrari 360 CS	1.22.3
Porsche GT3 RS	1.22.3
Corvette Z06	1.22.4
Noble M15	1.22.5
Lexus LFA	1.22.8 (wet)
Mercedes SL Black	1.23.0
Murcielago	1.23.7
Zonda	1.23.8
Koenigsegg	1.23.9
Aston Martin DBS	1.23.93
Veritas RS III	1.24.2
Prodrive P2	1.24.3
Audi R8	1.24.4
Aston Virage	1.24.4
TVR Sagaris	1.24.6
Mitsubishi Evo FQ400	1.24.8
TVR Tuscan	1.24.8
Bentley Continental Supersports	1.24.9
Porsche Boxster Spyder	1.24.9
Merc E63 AMG	1.24.9
Noble M400	1.25.0
BMW M1	1.25.0

Power Lap Car used	Time (mins)
Lotus Exige S	1.25.1
BMW M3 Saloon	1.25.3
Lamborghini Gallardo Spyder	1.25.7
Lotus Evora	1.25.7
Lamborghini Gallardo	1.25.8
BMW Z4 M	1.26.0
Porsche Cayman	1.26.2
Porsche 911 Carrera 2S	1.26.2
Brabus Biturbo Roadster	1.26.2
BMW M5	1.26.2
VXR Bathurst	1.26.3
Lotus Exige	1.26.4
BMW M3	1.26.5 (m)
Jaguar XFR	1.26.7
Chevrolet Corvette	1.26.8
Lexus IS-F	1.26.8
Mercedes CLS 55 AMG	1.26.9
Aston Martin Vanquish S	1.27.1
Aston Martin DB9	1.27.1
Holden Maloo	1.27.1
Telsa Roadster	1.27.2
Porsche 911 GT3	1.27.2
TVR 350C	1.27.5
Nissan 370Z	1.27.5
Audi RS5	1.27.5 (m)
Subaru Cossie	1.27.7 (w)
Camaro	1.27.9

Power Lap Car used	Time (mins)
BMW M3 CSL	1.28.0
Roush Mustang	1.28.0
Renault Megane R26R	1.28.1
BMW Z4	1.28.2
Marcos TSO GT2	1.28.2
Subaru WRX Sti	1.28.2
BMW X5M	1.28.2
Mitsubishi Evo X	1.28.22
Dodge Viper SRT-10	1.28.5
MG SV	1.28.6
Porsche 911 Carrera S	1.28.9
Mitsubishi Evo VIII	1.28.9
BMW Alpina Z8	1.29.0
Mercedes CL65	1.29.0
Ford Focus RS	1.29.3
VW Golf W12	1.29.6
Zenvo ST1	1.29.9 (very wet)
Alfa 3.7 GTA Autodelta	1.30.0
Ford Shelby GT500	1.30.0
Subaru Impreza STI	1.30.1
Vauxhall Monaro VXR	1.30.1
Aston Martin DB7 GT	1.30.4
Golf R32	1.30.4
Ford Focus RS 500	1.30.8 (w)
Audi S4	1.30.9
Porsche 911 Turbo	1.31.0
BMW 760Li	1.31.2

Power Lap Car used	Time (mins)
Vauxhall VX220 turbo	1.31.3
Vauxhall VXR8	1.31.3
New Audi TT	1.31.4
Honda NSX Type R	1.31.6
BMW M3	1.31.8
Nissan 350Z	1.31.8
Mazda RX-8	1.31.8
BMW 535d	1.31.8
BMW 130	1.31.9
Mercedes S63 AMG	1.32.0
Ford Focus RS	1.32.2
Mazda 6 MPS	1.32.2
Lotus Esprit V8	1.32.5
Audi TT V6	1.32.7
MG ZT	1.33.0
Noble M12 GTO	1.33.1
Mercedes SL 55 AMG	1.33.2
Volkswagen Golf R32	1.33.2
Audi Q7 V12 TDI	1.33.2
Cadillac CTS	1.33.3
Honda Civic Type-R	1.33.5
Holden Monaro	1.33.9
Ford Mondeo ST220	1.34.5
Jaguar XKR	1.34.7
Ford Focus ST	1.34.9
Volvo S60R	1.35.0
Ferrari 575M	1.35.2

Power Lap Car used	Time (mins)
Vauxhall Vectra VXR	1.35.3
Our Car	1.35.4
Fiat 500 Abarth	1.35.5
Alfa 147 GTA	1.35.6
Lotus Elise	1.35.6
Aston Martin Vanquish	1.36.2
Renault Clio V6	1.36.2
Honda Civic Type R	1.36.5
Alfa Romeo Brera	1.36.9
Saab 95 Aero	1.37.9
Maserati 3200 GT	1.38.0
Alfa Romeo 8C	1.38.2
Bowler Wildcat	1.39.4
Bentley Arnarge	1.40.8
Overfinch Range Rover	1.44.0
Aston Martin DB5	1.46.0
Hawk HF 3000	1.48.2
Porsche Paw Au Chocolat	18.37.00
1986 Porsche 959	DNF
1987 Ferrari F40	DNS

W / M = Times for a wet / moist course

DNF = Did Not Finish

DNS = Did Not Start

"what happened was a tragedy and that as much as I think he's a knob, I quite liked working with Jeremy".

James May

"Gutted at such a sad end to an era. We're all three of us idiots in our different ways but it's been an incredible ride together".

Richard Hammond

"At least we left 'em wanting more. And that alone, when you think about it, is quite an achievement for a show that started 13 years ago,"

Andi Wilman.

"In the meantime I'm getting really good at tennis. My forehand has improved immeasurably."

Jeremy Clarkson

"------------------------"

The Stig

26722466R00150

Made in the USA
Middletown, DE
06 December 2015